Let's Drink to Your Health!

NEW REVISED EDITION

A self-help guide to sensible drinking

Nick Heather and Ian Robertson

BPS
BOOKS

Published by The British Psychological Society

First published in 1986 by BPS Books (The British Psychological Society)
St Andrews House, 48 Princess Road East, Leicester LE1 7DR, UK.
Reprinted 1987, 1995
New revised edition 1996

A catalogue record for this book is available from the British Library.

ISBN 1 85433 206 6

Set in Melior by Patrick Armstrong, Book Production Services,
28a Grove Vale, London SE22 8DY

Printed and bound in Great Britain by Biddles Ltd, Guildford, Surrey GU1 1DA

CONTENTS

ACKNOWLEDGEMENTS

The authors are extremely grateful to Anna Luce for help in the preparation of this revised edition. We are also grateful to the following for helpful advice on various sections of the book: Dr Chris Day, Eileen Goddard, Christine Godfrey. We are especially grateful to Dr Moira Plant for detailed comments and suggestions on Chapter 5. Needless to say, all opinions and errors remain our responsibility.

1
TOWARDS HEALTHIER DRINKING

Do you enjoy a drink?

There is absolutely no reason why you shouldn't. You are merely joining the billions of people who, ever since stone-age men and women first drank fermented honey, have enjoyed the fruits of fermentation – the well-known chemical process which, with the help of yeast, converts sugar into ethyl alcohol.

The aim of this book is to help you enjoy alcohol's benefits while avoiding the problems it can cause. For alcohol *does* have many positive effects; it inspires song and verse, seals bargains, cements friendships and is the ceremonial oil for many a rusty social occasion. Alcohol is our favourite drug and our most dangerous one.

In Britain today, only a minority of adults abstain totally from alcohol. People who choose not to drink have made a decision which is perfectly sensible for them. However, those of us who do drink – including the authors – are faced with the challenge of finding a healthy and enjoyable pattern of drinking. That is what we will try to help you do in the following pages.

This book is not for alcoholics

One kind of person whose drinking is obviously doing them harm is known as an 'alcoholic'. If you think you are an alcoholic, then this book is definitely *not* for you.

We had better explain what we mean by an alcoholic. It is somebody who is an 'alcohol addict'. In other words, it is somebody who usually drinks very large amounts of alcohol and suffers from withdrawal symptoms when drinking stops.

1

Withdrawal symptoms can include a number of unpleasant experiences, including shakiness, feeling very agitated, sweating profusely, or feeling frightened and depressed after stopping drinking. In extreme cases, fits or hallucinations can occur. All these are caused by the fact that your body has become accustomed to the presence of alcohol and has come to depend on it to carry out its normal functioning. In this way, alcoholics are said to be 'physically dependent' on alcohol. Therefore, when alcohol is removed, the body 'complains' about it in the form of withdrawal symptoms.

Withdrawal symptoms can be very painful and unpleasant and often the only way the sufferer can think of to get rid of them, or avoid them happening in the first place, is to have more to drink. This creates a vicious circle, with heavy drinking to avoid withdrawal symptoms, which in turn produces more withdrawal symptoms, and so on. This vicious circle is very hard to break without medical assistance and if you have experienced withdrawal symptoms recently you are physically dependent on alcohol and you should seek help by consulting the list of addresses given at the end of this book (Appendix A) or by going to your family doctor without delay. To repeat, **this book is not for alcoholics**

So who is this book intended for?

The answer to this is **anyone whose drinking is causing them problems.** By this we simply mean a person who has not yet reached the stage of drinking to avoid or reduce withdrawal symptoms, but who is nevertheless doing himself or herself harm through drinking too much. It is important to understand that the harm caused by excessive drinking can be of many different kinds.

Health. Drinking too much can harm your health in many different ways. You probably know that whenever you have too much to drink you are risking damage to your liver. But the workings of your brain can also be affected by regular intake of large amounts, and heavy drinking can make you overweight. There are many, many ways in which excessive drinking can attack your general fitness and health, and we discuss some of these in more detail in Chapter 4.

2

Work. Your performance at work may be affected for the worse because you are hungover in the morning. Or you may miss work completely because of the previous night's drinking. Maybe those few drinks at lunchtime make you a bit drowsy and inefficient in the afternoon.

Money. You may be spending more on drink than you or your family can reasonably afford. Money spent on alcohol could be used for other, more essential items.

The Law. You may have got into trouble with the police because of the way you behave when drunk. And, of course, if you drink and drive, you are taking stupid and unnecessary risks with your own and other people's lives.

Social life. You may find that some of your friends are less keen on your company than they used to be, because you have offended them when you were drunk. People may be avoiding you because you have ceased to be amusing. Or your whole social life may have become centred on the pub, to the exclusion of all the other worthwhile things you used to do.

Family. Your drinking may have caused quarrels between you and your wife or husband, and your marriage may have been jeopardized in this way. Or you may have been paying less attention to your children than you should. There are many ways in which your family life may be spoiled by drinking too often and too much.

Fights and accidents. Heavy drinkers sometimes get into fights they wouldn't dream of becoming involved in if they were sober. Also, your chances of having an accident, at work or elsewhere, are greatly increased by excessive drinking.

Other problems. As well as these kinds of trouble, you may have problems which are not actually *caused* by alcohol but which are made worse by drinking too much – where your drinking is preventing you from finding a solution to the problem. Try and think if this applies to you.

3

What is a drinking problem?

You sometimes hear heavy drinkers say: 'I'm not an alcoholic. I don't have a drink problem'. There is a lot of confusion here. You may not be an alcoholic in the sense we have used the term in this book – as being physically dependent on alcohol. But if you recognize any of the types of harm just described as applying to you, then let there be no mistake about it, *you do have a problem with alcohol.* All this means is the presence of some problem, *any* problem, connected in some way with your drinking. And if you have such a problem then, obviously, you should do something about it.

This book has been written to help you do something about it. There is no magical solution to a drinking problem and we cannot guarantee results simply from reading this book. The effort and the determination has to come from you, and the book is intended merely to help you to help yourself. This is why we have called it a *self-help guide.*

At the same time, however, solving a problem with alcohol is much more than simply a question of 'will power'. Scientific research has shown that if you use certainkinds of methods in the attempt to bring your behaviour under control you are more likely to succeed. This book is based on results of this research and is aimed at teaching you the best methods to use to reduce your drinking. Also, you may have tried to cut down in the past and failed. This was probably because you lacked a *system* for cutting down. This book shows you how to approach the problem systematically. Rather than 'will power', this book will teach you 'skill power'.

Note that this is not a book which is just to be read and passively accepted. Rather, it is a 'doing' book which sets you exercises to complete and skills to practise. It therefore requires your most active participation.

Who should stop drinking completely?

You may have been under the impression that the only solution to an alcohol problem is to give up drinking completely.

This is not true. It has been conclusively shown that many problem drinkers are able to reduce their consumption to amounts which no longer do them harm. However, there are circumstances in which you should not attempt to control your drinking but *should* decide to abstain altogether. These are:

- If you have had a drinking problem in the past and solved it by total abstinence, then you should not be tempted by the contents of this book to return to drinking. Even if you feel you would occasionally enjoy a drink, the risk involved cannot justify upsetting your successful adjustment to life.

- If you have already suffered permanent medical damage from excessive drinking, then it would clearly be very foolish to continue drinking in any amounts. You should also abstain if there is *any* other medical reason, not necessarily connected with alcohol, why you should not drink. We go into some of these reasons in Chapter 4 but, meanwhile, if you suspect that you should not drink on medical grounds, consult your doctor.

- You may simply decide you cannot be bothered with further drinking and that you would stand a better chance of solving your problems, and enjoying life more fully, by cutting out alcohol. You must weigh up the advantages and disadvantages of stopping completely as against continuing to drink. If you feel a preference for abstinence, do not let anything we have written here put you off.

- Heavy drinking by pregnant women may harm the unborn child. Perhaps the simplest option is not to drink at all when you are pregnant. We discuss this issue in more detail in Chapter 5.

Why all the fuss about alcohol?

Well, to begin with, people have been fussing about it for tens of thousands of years, so why stop now? As soon as Noah was able to leave the Ark, the book of Genesis reports: 'Noah began to be a husbandman, and he planted a vineyard. And he drank of the wine and was drunken'.

So begins our long history of concern about alcohol and its effects. Even in the Babylonia of 1700BC, the Code of Hammurbai stipulated a variety of restrictions on the sale and consumption of alcohol. The enthusiastic Chinese Emperor, Chung K'iang, took things somewhat further by executing drunkards as a public remonstrance.

And so on until 18th century Britain when the Industrial Revolution drained the countryside of peasant farmers and herded them into the 'dark Satanic mills' of the great cities. Hitherto, alcohol had been drunk in very large quantities, but was meshed into the leisurely pace of rural life, where it did not interfere with the work cycle. Now, with factories requiring workers to keep regular hours and operate complicated machines, the potentially disruptive effects of alcohol became obvious. This, tied to the fact that alcohol – in particular Dutch gin – was creating havoc among the new city-dwellers, led to the development of a strong temperance movement, which vigorously campaigned against 'the demon drink'. The religious revivalism with which this movement became associated, with its moralistic approach to alcohol use, has had a profound influence to this day on our attitudes to alcohol and its problems.

At the end of World War I, the USA was about to introduce prohibition and the city of Dundee would soon send Winston Churchill scuttling back to London after losing an election to Britain's first Temperance MP. Alcohol consumption – and hence the rate of alcohol problems – began its final decline until it reached its lowest point since records were kept, just after World War II. From the gin-swilling debauchery of Hogarth's 18th century London to the relatively prim sobriety of post-war Britain, drinking has been steadily increasing in more recent times.We reached a plateau in the 1980s and drinking has not increased since then. Nevertheless, as a nation we now drink roughly twice as much as we did 40 years ago and this is nearly as much as the very high levels recorded at the beginning of the century. Although this may be a pale shadow of the huge quantities consumed in the reign of the Georges, it has led to significant increases in the scale of problems caused by alcohol.

7

- Despite the fact that alcohol consumption remained roughly the same, deaths due to alcoholic liver cirrhosis increased by 25 per cent from 1980 to 1992.

- In 1992, 33 per cent of pedestrians, 26 per cent of motorbike riders and 17 per cent of car users killed in road accidents were over the legal alcohol limit.

- Hospital diagnoses of 'alcoholism' have more than doubled over the last 25 years.

- Convictions for drink driving have more than trebled since 1968, when the breath test was introduced.

- As a rough estimate five times as many people in Britain are now experiencing serious problems relating in some way to their drinking than in the early 1960s.

- In 1994, 27 per cent of men and 11 per cent of women were drinking over the levels for 'sensible' drinking recommended by doctors.

More statistics could be quoted. The simple and unavoidable fact is that the more you drink, the more chance you have of running into problems. This is as true for nations as it is for individuals. The total amount of alcohol consumed in different countries is closely related to the number of alcohol problems of various kinds which will be found there. And in the same country over time, the number of alcohol problems recorded is closely linked to changes in how much alcohol is being drunk.

Two special groups of the population have shown increases in consumption and problems which are greater than the average – women and young people. As this suggests, it is young women in particular who have shown the greatest change of all in their drinking habits. We devote the whole of Chapter 5 of this book to the important topic of 'Women and Alcohol'.

Lying behind all the increases in consumption and in problems is the fact that alcohol has become progressively cheaper in real terms over the last 40 or 50 years. Many people are surprised when they hear this, possibly because of confusion with the actual, rather than the inflation-adjusted price and because of romantic nostalgia for the past. But if inflation is taken fully into account, the price of alcoholic drinks of all kinds can be shown to have fallen dramatically since the last war, especially when compared with necessities like food.

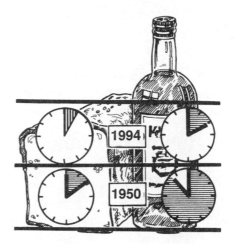

Time taken to earn the money for a loaf of bread compared to a bottle of whisky in 1950 and in 1994.

For instance, in 1950 it took the average manual worker just under nine minutes to earn the wherewithal for a loaf of bread, whereas in 1994 it took five minutes. However, in 1950 a bottle of whisky took over $10\frac{1}{2}$ hours to earn, compared with less than two hours in 1994. These changes are illustrated in the diagram. The important point is that, **the cheaper alcohol is, the more we will avail ourselves of it.**

All these facts and figures do not mean that alcohol is an unmitigated evil and should be banned. Cars cause thousands of deaths, but the 'ban cars' lobby is not a big one. Most sensible people advocate safer roads and safer driving. In the same way, this book urges safer drinking. Alcohol, like the motor car, is a great blessing when it is used properly.

We hope we have communicated to you the fact that we are not trying to be killjoys. We know that drinking can be a most enjoyable thing to do, and this is why we have stressed the pleasures and benefits alcohol can bring. We are also aware that some people who are drinking too much, according to the definitions given in this book, will decide to ignore our advice and carry on the way they are. They are, of course, perfectly entitled to do so. This is a free country and it is up to you to decide how much you want to drink. All we insist on is two things.

First, in making the choice of how much you should aim to drink, you should be fully informed of the facts which bear on that choice.

Second, if you do decide to try to cut down, you should do so in the most efficient manner possible by following the hints given in this book.

How to use this book

As we said before, this is a 'doing' book and there are lots of sections where you are asked to fill in spaces with information which applies to you. Although this information is not especially embarrassing, we would quite understand if you felt that you didn't want anyone else to read it. In that case, you should obviously keep the book in a place where others are not likely to come across it. But, whether or not you wish to keep your entries in the book private, it is essential that you fill in all the spaces provided if you are to obtain any benefit.

Other parts of the book provide you with facts about alcohol and drinking, and we have set you a few questions to see how many of these facts you have learned. You are best advised not to continue until you have got all the quiz answers correct. Even where there are no quizzes, you should make sure you have understood everything before moving on.

The most important thing to remember about using this self-help guide is that it is not just a book which is to be read once and then thrown aside. Rather, we suggest you use it over a period of months, maybe even years. You will need to go through it slowly, making sure you have filled in all the required spaces and practised all the exercises. After finishing the book, you should keep it in a handy place so that you can keep coming back to it to remind yourself about important conclusions.

To summarize what we have covered in this chapter:

- if you are not physically dependent on alcohol
- if you do have some sort of problem with your drinking
- if you have seriously made up your mind to do something about it
- if you are not one of those people best advised to stop drinking completely
- if you want to enjoy your drinking in a way which does you no harm

then this book is for **you.**

2
WHY SHOULD I CUT DOWN?

If you have reached this far in the book, you presumably feel that you *do* have some sort of problem with your drinking and wish to do something about it. The purpose of this chapter is to make clear exactly what *kind* of problem you have, so that you can tackle it more effectively.

*   *   *   *   *

Do you really know how much you drink?

The most obvious kind of drinking problem has to do with the amount you drink. You may simply have the feeling that you are drinking more than is good for your health. Let us see if you are right!

The first thing we have to do is to convert everything you drink into *standard units* of alcohol. A standard unit will contain roughly one half ounce (or 8 grammes) of pure ethyl alcohol. The basic rule is:

one unit = one half pint of beer

To change what you drink into standard units, use the conversion table.

Note that the most common mistake in guessing the strength of different drinks is to underestimate the strength of beer. And one of the commonest fallacies about drinking is to think that sticking to beer can't do you any harm. Just to stress the point:

one half pint of beer = one whisky = 1 unit

one pint of beer = two whiskies = 2 units

CONVERSION TABLE

DRINK	UNITS
1 pub measure (1/6 gill) of spirits (whisky, gin, vodka)	1
1 glass of fortified wine (sherry, martini, port)	1
1 glass of table wine (depending on strength)	1-2*
1 pint of beer or lager (depending on strength)	2-3**
1 pint low alcohol beer	$^1/_3$
1 pint cider (depending on strength)	2-4***
1 can of beer or lager	$1^1/_2$
1 bottle of 'super' or 'special' lager	$2^1/_2$
1 can of 'super' or 'special' lager	4
1 bottle of table wine (depending on strength)	7-12*
1 litre bottle of table wine (depending on strength)	10-18*
1 bottle of fortified wine (sherry, martini, port)	14
1 bottle of spirits (whisky, gin, vodka)	30
1 glass or can of 'alcoholic lemonade'	2

* Wines vary considerably in strength. Some sparkling wines, for instance, contain up to 2 units per glass. If in doubt, check the alcohol content on the label: wine of strength 1 unit per glass will contain between 8% and 11% alcohol, whereas the stronger wines will be around 15% alcohol.

** Lighter beers and some lagers are about 2 units per pint. Some heavier beers, such as Guinness and some 'real ales', contain nearer 3 units per pint. Certain draught lagers, such as Beck's and Stella Artois, are also nearer 3 units per pint. Occasionally, you get beers and lagers which are even stronger than this.

* * *Light ciders, such as Woodpecker and Autumn Gold, are just over 2 units per pint. Stronger cider, such as Blackthorn and Strongbow, contain nearly 4 units per pint.

Now, we want you to think about how much you had to drink during the last typical week.

First, think about what you had in the seven days just past. If that week was roughly typical of your drinking, it is the week we need. If it was not, try to remember the most recent week which *was* typical – without going so far back in the past that you can't remember what happened.

Using the chart on page 16 we want you to try to recall what you had to drink during this typical week. If today is Tuesday, Day 1 on the chart would be last Tuesday, Day 2 would be last Wednesday and so on, until you come to Day 7, which would, of course, be yesterday. To help you remember, we have divided up each day into three parts and we have also left spaces for you to write down where and with whom you were drinking. This will help you to calculate the number of units of alcohol you drank during each part of the day. As an example, a day from the chart might look like this:

A Typical Week's Drinking

Day	When	Where	What	With whom	Units	Total
Saturday	Morning	Nag's Head	1 pint bitter	Simon	2	
	Afternoon	Simon's House	2 cans lager	Simon Mary, John	3	9
	Evening	The Bull	2 large whiskies	John	4	

Before you fill in the chart, a word of warning. Surveys have proved that if heavy drinkers are asked in an interview how much they drink, there is a strong possibility that they will report less than the true amounts. These heavy drinkers may be kidding themselves as well as the interviewer. So, be on your guard against completing the chart with quantities which are less than you really drank on the days in question. Try to be as honest with yourself as you possibly can. After all, there will be only one loser if you are not completely frank – yourself!

Another point to remember is that the drinks of spirits or wine you may have at home are often bigger than you would get in a pub. And a pub measure is what we are using for our standard unit of alcohol. So, to calculate what you have drunk at home during the last typical week, you will need to estimate how many pub measures were poured for each glass.

"Laissez faire and let laissez faire is what I believe in."

A simple exercise may help here. If you own a measuring glass, use that to practise pouring out a standard unit, or two if you prefer. First pour a drink into an unmarked glass, then transfer it to the measuring glass to see how accurate you have been. Then carry on until you get it about right. If you were pouring spirits, you should have poured one fluid ounce for a single unit, if ordinary table wine it should be 4 fluid ounces, and if fortified wine (i.e. sherry, port or martini) it should be $2^1/_2$ fluid ounces. This exercise will help you to calculate bet ter how much you had to drink during the last typical week, and will also help you to monitor your consumption more accurately in the future.

Now fill in the chart. When you have added up the units of alcohol during each day, enter the total in the right-hand column of the chart. Then add up all seven totals to arrive at the Grand Total for the week. This is the all-important figure. We

A Typical Week's Drinking

Day	When	Where	What	Who with	Units	Total

Total for week

are now in a position to say if you are drinking too much alcohol and need to cut down for that reason alone. However, **the crucial figures are different for men and for women.**

MEN

If your Grand Total for the week is more than 21 units,

You Are At Increased Risk Of Harm From Drinking And You Are Advised To Cut Down

WOMEN

If your Grand Total for the week is more than 14 units,

You Are At Increased Risk Of Harm From Drinking And You Are Advised To Cut Down

These are guidelines for sensible drinking. There are three reasons for using these particular guidelines. Scientific research has shown that if you drink more than these amounts:

1. **You increase your chances of damaging your health through drinking.**

2. **You increase the risk of other kinds of harm through drinking (psychological and social harm to yourself and others).**

3. **You increase the risk of becoming physically dependent on alcohol.**

The reason for having a lower limit for women than for men is that women are more at risk for these reasons. We will go into this in more detail in Chapter 5.

The reader may be aware that, just before Christmas 1995, the Government issued a report entitled 'Sensible Drinking'. Although the advice given to the public in this report was complicated, it was widely interpreted as suggesting that limits for sensible drinking would be raised from 21 units to 28 units per week for men and from 14 units to 21 units a week for women. This was in direct contradiction to the evidence the Government had received from leading doctors and other experts all over Britain (including the British Medical Association and the three Royal Colleges of Physicians, of Psychiatrists and of General Practitioners). These experts all strongly argued that the recommended drinking levels should be kept where they were; that is, at 21 units per week for men and 14 units per week for women. In this book, therefore, we have chosen to ignore the Government's views on this matter and stick with the previous recommended levels. It is true that there is some overall benefit from moderate – very moderate – drinking and we will deal with this issue later. But the evidence quite clearly shows that drinking above the levels we have given, and recommended by nearly all doctors, is linked with an increased risk of medical damage.

You may be saying to yourself that these limits are ridiculous because everybody you know, including yourself, drinks more than the weekly amounts we have given. If you are saying this, then all it proves is that your friends are drinking too much as well as you! The point is that some local communities or groups of friends drink a lot more than others, and your community or group may be one of them. So don't be surprised if large numbers of people you know are drinking more than is good for their health. It happens only too often.

You may also be saying to yourself that several people you know have been drinking more than our 'sensible limits' for years and have not come to any harm. This is a very familiar kind of argument and is often trotted out in relation to smoking and lung cancer. You know the sort of thing: 'My Uncle Fred smoked 40 a day all his life and lived till 80'. This is based on a simple misunderstanding of the nature of health risks. The point is that they are just that – risks! The fact that you smoke 40 a day does not mean that it is inevitable that you will die of lung cancer or that you will not be able to find examples of heavy smokers who have been lucky enough to escape the disease. What it does mean is that you considerably increase your chances of getting lung cancer, to the point where the risk is simply not acceptable.

Exactly the same is true of heavy drinking – if you drink more than the limits we have given, *you are increasing the risk of damaging your health.* As you might expect, the more you drink, the greater the risk becomes. For example, men drinking over 50 units per week and women drinking over 35 units per week have reached a level of very high risk, where the chance of some kind of harm is almost certain. As we said before, it is a free country and you are entitled to gamble with your health if you so desire. But you should be aware of what the risks are. For example, if you are a heavy drinker, then compared with light drinkers and abstainers:

- You are twice as likely to die of heart disease.

- You are twice as likely to die of cancer.

- You are twelve times as likely to die of cirrhosis of the liver.

- You are three times as likely to die in a car crash.

- You are six times as likely to commit suicide.

For all these reasons, if you suspect you may be drinking too much, but are not sure whether you can make the effort to cut down, just pause and **think what may happen if you do not.**

More about the limits

It is also important to make clear that, even if your weekly Grand Total is lower than the limit, this does not necessarily mean that your drinking is completely safe. And it certainly does *not* mean that you should increase your drinking up to the limit. In fact, there is no limit which is completely safe for everyone. For one thing, young people who have only recently started drinking may be less able to handle alcohol and weekly amounts below the limit may still be too much for them. For another thing, your Grand Total over the week may be lower than the limits, but you may still have drunk too much on one or two occasions during that week. The limit does not mean you are free to drink it all in one night!

Remember also that no level of alcohol consumption is completely safe in all circumstances. For example, there are occasions when even one or two drinks can be too much – such as when you intend to operate machinery or drive a motor vehicle. In fact, our advice is that **you should not drink at all before driving** because any amount of alcohol impairs your performance and increases the risk of accidents. And it can also be dangerous to drink any alcohol if you are taking some kinds of medicine.

Finally, it is better not to drink every day but to have one or two days per week completely free from alcohol. This gives your body the chance to recover from the effects of alcohol.

What other reasons are there for cutting down?

Even if your intake is fairly evenly spread and your weekly Grand Total is under the limit, you could still have a problem with your drinking. Remember that this is *any* problem connected with alcohol. For example, keeping to the weekly 'healthy' limit might be unsafe if you drove your car after drinking. You might not feel drunk, but you would still risk being arrested for drink driving. Therefore, you *would* have a problem.

On the next page you will find a list of questions connected with your drinking in the last three months. If you answer 'yes' to any of these questions then, irrespective of how much you drink, that is a reason for cutting down which applies to you.

There is another purpose in adding to the list of problems for you to check. The problems relating just to the amount you drink – the increased chances of damaging your health and becoming dependent on alcohol – are not immediately obvious problems. You may not be able to actually see or feel anything going wrong. For this reason, you may not be convinced there is a problem to be solved. This is why we have included an extra list of problems connected with drinking which have more immediate and obvious consequences. As well as the amount you drink, you should also pay attention to the other kinds of problems which are likely to occur.

Now read these questions and put a circle round the answers which apply to you. If you answer 'yes' to any of them, drink is causing problems in your life and you do have a reason for cutting down.

DURING THE LAST THREE MONTHS

Have you woken up and been unable to remember some of the things you had done while drinking the previous night?	Yes	No
Have you been in arguments with your family or friends because of your drinking?	Yes	No
Have you found that your hands were shaking in the morning after drinking the previous evening?	Yes	No
Has your work suffered in any way because of drinking?	Yes	No
Have you found yourself neglecting any of your responsibilities because of drinking?	Yes	No
Have you had a drink first thing in the morning to steady your nerves or get rid of a hangover?	Yes	No
Has there been any occasion when you have felt unable to stop drinking?	Yes	No
Have you feared that you were becoming dependent on alcohol?	Yes	No
Have you needed a drink to face certain situations or problems?	Yes	No
Have you had financial difficulties because of drink?	Yes	No
Have you given up hobbies, sport or other interests and spent more time drinking instead?	Yes	No
Have you concealed the amount you drink from those close to you?	Yes	No
Have you been drunk for several days running?	Yes	No
Have you been violent after drinking?	Yes	No
Have you been arrested for drunkenness?	Yes	No

If you have answered 'yes' to any of these questions, drink is causing you problems and you do have a reason for cutting down. So carry on reading.

Your reasons for cutting down

Now is the time to collect together all the reasons for cutting down which apply to you. Write them in the spaces provided. If you can think of any good reason for cutting down which is important to you but which we have forgotten to mention, write that down too. Put each reason on a separate line and use as many lines as you need.

I shall cut down because ...

Reason one

Reason two

Reason three

Reason four

Reason five

Reason six

It's all up to you

We presume that you have definitely decided to cut down your drinking and that you have discovered the reasons for doing so which apply to you. We must now repeat something we mentioned for the first time in Chapter 1.

There is no magical solution to cutting down your drinking. Nobody can do it for you. The effort and the determination has to come from you.

This is why you should now pause and think carefully about the effort you will have to make. You must make up your mind not to be put off by difficulties and not to be discouraged if you do not succeed at first. Remember Robert the Bruce and the spider!

To help you summon up the determination which is needed, we are going to ask you to do something which may seem a little strange at first. But we know that it will be helpful to you in your attempts to cut down.

Make a contract with yourself.

Make a promise to try your best to cut down your drinking, sign it and date it. Then you will always have it to refer back to when you begin to lose heart. **Do it now!**

A
CONTRACT
WITH MYSELF

I promise that I shall try the hardest I can to cut down my drinking so that it no longer does me harm

SIGNED

DATE

3
HOW DOES ALCOHOL AFFECT ME?

Having discovered why you should cut down your drinking, you now need to understand how alcohol affects you. But first try the quiz to find out how much you already know. If you get any of the answers wrong, come back to the quiz after reading this chapter and correct any misunderstandings you may have had about the effects of alcohol.

Q-U-I-Z

1. Abuse of alcohol causes as much damage in society as heroin and other hard drugs. ☐ *True* ☐ *False*

2. Alcohol is a stimulant drug. ☐ *True* ☐ *False*

3. Alcohol will warm you up on a cold day.
☐ *True* ☐ *False*

4. Alcohol can kill you by stopping your breathing.
☐ *True* ☐ *False*

5. Alcohol spreads through your body very slowly.
☐ *True* ☐ *False*

6. Only the liver removes alcohol from the bloodstream. ☐ *True* ☐ *False*

7. Alcohol contains... ☐ *Proteins* ☐ *Carbohydrates*
☐ *Vitamins*

8. How long does it take your body to get rid of the alcohol in two pints of beer? ☐ *Two hours*
☐ *Three hours* ☐ *Four hours*

9. You can sober up by...
☐ *Drinking lots of black coffee*
☐ *Taking a cold shower* ☐ *Getting some fresh air.*

10. Drinking spirits is more dangerous than beer.
☐ *True* ☐ *False*

A 1. False. It causes many times more damage. 2. False. It is a depressant drug. 3. False. It takes heat away from the body. 4. True. But only after drinking very large amounts very rapidly 5. False. It takes only a few minutes. 6. True. For all practical purposes. 7. No. No. No 8. Four Hours. 9. All false. Only time can sober you up. 10. False. Remember, a half-pint of beer is just as strong as one measure of spirits.

Alcohol is a drug

We all know that heroin, cocaine, cannabis and LSD are drugs. But it is amazing how many people do not understand that alcohol is a drug too – and a powerful one at that.

The most obvious difference between alcohol and the other drugs just mentioned is that alcohol is legal whereas the others are not. But, make no mistake about it, **misuse of alcohol causes many times more damage in society than all those illegal drugs put together.** There is a great deal of concern at present about heroin abuse, especially among young people. This is, indeed, a justifiable concern, but it should not obscure the fact that the number of deaths per year caused by heroin pales into insignificance when compared to the number of deaths due to excessive drinking.

It is worth noting what kind of drug alcohol is. It is a *depressant* drug. This means that it dulls the workings of the brain and is the same type of drug as the barbiturates which were once used as sleeping pills. Depressant drugs may make you lose some of your inhibitions and also lower your efficiency at tasks involving co-ordinated movements – like driving a car and many skills you may perform at work.

You may be surprised to learn that alcohol is a depressant drug because you have always thought of it as a stimulant. This is because it may *feel* like a stimulant at first, but this 'stimulant' effect is only short-lived, as anyone who drinks alcohol must know.

Incidentally, mixing alcohol with other drugs can be very dangerous and is definitely not to be recommended. This includes drugs prescribed by a doctor, like sleeping pills, tranquillizers, slimming pills, anti-histamines and cough medicines. We go into this in a bit more detail in the next chapter.

Like other drugs, alcohol is a deadly poison if taken in too large doses. It can cause death by knocking out the part of the brain which controls breathing. However, you have to drink a lot of alcohol in a very short space of time for this to happen and the event is fortunately rare. It usually happens as a result of stupid drinking bets, but can also occur when alcohol is consumed after taking sleeping pills.

. . . it fills you full of pep and zip and go go go!

Makes you warble like a nightingale gone mad.

It's great stuff all right . . .

HARGREAVES

. . . but you feel terrible when it wears off.

What happens to your body when you drink alcohol?

After being swallowed, alcohol travels to the stomach where about one fifth of it is absorbed into the bloodstream. (Unlike most other things you take in, it is not necessary for the body to digest alcohol; it can go to work straight away in the same form in which you drank it.) The rest of the alcohol is absorbed through the small intestine and into the blood. Only minutes after you drink, there will be alcohol in every part of your body.

There are certain things which slow down or speed up the rate at which alcohol is absorbed into the bloodstream and this will affect how quickly you begin to feel drunk. If you drink on an empty stomach, the alcohol will travel through your body much more rapidly than if you have recently had a meal. On the other hand, if there is food in the stomach, it will be absorbed more slowly and you will not get intoxicated so quickly.

It is true that the other ingredients in beer slow down the rate of alcohol absorption, so that intoxication is slower with beer than spirits. (But, as we have explained previously, this does not mean that beer is 'safer' than spirits.) In the opposite direction, the bubbles in champagne and other sparkling wines speed up the passage of alcohol into the bloodstream so you feel the effects more quickly. This is also true of the gas in ginger ale, tonic or soda water. Indeed, in the average gin and tonic, mankind has devised about the most efficient means possible of getting alcohol into the bloodstream, short of actually injecting it into the veins!

It is when alcohol reaches the brain, of course, that things start to happen. As we explained before, alcohol dulls the action of the brain and, although this may feel stimulating at first, it actually has a depressant effect. This effect starts with the highest centres of the brain's activity and then works its way downwards, with more and more drastic effects.

Another fallacy which should be mentioned is the one which says that alcohol warms you up on a cold day. It does not! It is true that there is an immediate feeling of warmth after drinking, because of a raised pulse and blood pressure. But this actually takes heat away from the body, so that, if you are ever stranded in freezing conditions, drinking alcohol is not a good thing to do. So ignore that Saint Bernard dog!

How does your body get rid of alcohol?

Less than one tenth of the alcohol you take in is eliminated through the urine and breath. The rest of it has to be burnt up by the body in a process known as 'oxidation'. Other food substances can be oxidized in tissues throughout the body, but virtually the only place alcohol can be burnt up is the liver. This is why the liver is one of the first parts of the body to suffer from excessive drinking, as we shall see in Chapter 4.

Alcohol is oxidized by the liver very slowly. In fact, it takes the liver about one hour to burn up one standard unit of alcohol – roughly equal to a single whisky or a half pint of beer (see page 12). This slow rate at which the body metabolizes alcohol means that it remains in the system long after you have finished drinking. Did you know that, depending on how much you have had, you can still fail a breathalyser test 24 hours after stopping drinking? This is why you should be very careful about driving the morning after you have been drinking heavily. For example, after seven pints of beer in an evening, you will probably still be over the legal limit for driving eight hours later!

This is also why drinking at lunchtime and again after work can get you into trouble. For example, if you have a 'liquid lunch' of three pints of beer, then have one more after work with your colleagues before driving home, you will almost certainly be over the legal driving limit. This is because the alcohol you had at lunchtime has not yet been metabolized by the time you start drinking again – you are simply topping up the level of alcohol in your blood.

By the way, drinking black coffee, having a cold shower or getting some fresh air do not sober you up. At best, they may help you to feel less drowsy, but they do not actually affect the level of alcohol in your blood. Nothing sobers you up except time.

In the liver alcohol is turned into a source of energy which can be used by all the body tissues. Thus, it is true that alcohol is a food. But it is a food which has no nutritional value. Other ingredients of beer and wine may have some nutritional value, but alcohol itself has none. And, of course, alcohol can make you fat and cause havoc with your diet. The many ways in which this can lead to ill health are discussed in the following chapter.

Hangovers

Most hangover cures are worthless. 'Prairie oysters' and similar recipes have not stood the test of laboratory experiments. Hangovers are caused in part by impurities or 'congeners' in alcoholic drinks, partly by dehydration, and partly by low blood sugar. Some experts think that hangover symptoms are nothing more than minor symptoms of withdrawal from alcohol. Part of what you feel when hungover might also be caused by over-stretching yourself while under the influence – too much talking/singing/dancing/ arguing, etc.

As a general rule, the darker a drink is, the more chance there is that it will cause a hangover. Thus brandy tends to produce more headaches than vodka, red wine more than white. This is because the darker liquids have more 'congeners' in them – though it is not clearly understood why they make you feel bad.

"We aim to grow absolutely everything we need to put in Pimm's." © Harpur

Those of you who have experienced the 'dry horrors' will not have to be told that alcohol dehydrates you, and dehydration can lead to headaches and other unpleasant symptoms. Alcohol is a diuretic – that is, it makes you urinate more than normal and over a night's drinking your body will lose more water than it absorbs. Thus, some people find that drinking a great deal of water before going to sleep helps to avoid hangovers.

Drugged sleep is bad sleep, and a hangover may be partly due to tiredness because of deep, unrestful, dreamless sleep (see page 54). Low blood sugar on top of this can make these symptoms worse. Rest and eating are the best answers here, and if nausea is dulling the appetite, bicarbonate of soda may help. Some people find that raw root ginger slowly chewed can relieve nausea.

Finally, it need hardly be added that there is one hangover cure which is very dangerous: 'hair of the dog' may be effective in the short term but is a very risky step which can lead to severe dependence upon alcohol. So, never drink alcohol the next morning. And remember, as we pointed out earlier, you can still be intoxicated many hours into the next day if you drank a lot the night before. For instance, if you are of average weight, and drank 12 units of alcohol between 10 p.m. and 2 a.m., at 12 noon the next day you would still have alcohol in your system! And that is just six pints of beer! If you had twice that amount, you would still have alcohol in your blood at 5 o'clock in the afternoon. So drink slowly and wisely: that is the best advice to avoid hangovers.

How much alcohol is there in different drinks?

In the last chapter, we explained the various strengths of different drinks, such as those you would normally order in a pub. We gave you a table for converting what you drank into standard units of alcohol (see page 13).

We are concerned here with something slightly different – the proportion of alcohol compared with other ingredients in various kinds of alcoholic drink, like beer, wine, sherry, gin, whisky, etc. You have probably seen '70° proof' on the label of a bottle of whisky and you may think this means that whisky contains 70 per cent alcohol.

Actually, whisky contains only about 40 per cent alcohol. The reason it is described as 70° (degrees) proof is that it contains 70 per cent of the amount of alcohol which would be needed for the mixture to catch fire if gunpowder were added to it, an amount roughly equivalent to 57 per cent of the total volume. This was the method used in times gone by as 'proof' that the mixture contained enough alcohol. You will find below a list of typical alcoholic drinks with a note of the 'proof' of the mixture and the approximate percentage of alcohol they actually contain.

HOW MUCH ALCOHOL IS THERE IN DIFFERENT DRINKS?

	° proof	per cent alcohol
Beer, Cider	8-12	4-6
Special strong beer and cider	12-16	6-8
Wine	14-27	8-15
Sherry, port, vermouth etc.	35	20
Spirits	70	40

Fortunately there is a trend these days to describe the alcohol content of drinks by the much simpler method of percentage alcohol by volume or %v/v (i.e., the actual percentage of alcohol in the drink). An EC Directive in 1989 made it a legal requirement for alcohol manufacturers to include %v/v on all drink labels. This avoids the old-fashioned and confusing 'proof' method.

Blood alcohol concentration

Having established how much alcohol different kinds of drink contain, we must now think about the intoxicating effects of alcohol. How drunk you are at any given time will depend on the amount of alcohol in your bloodstream. This is called the *Blood Alcohol Concentration*.

Alcohol is also present in your breath, and modern police roadside tests for drink driving measure breath alcohol.

However, this is closely related to the Blood Alcohol Concentration, or BAC for short.

It is important to understand BACs if you are going to cut down your drinking. You can use your knowledge of them to select what BAC you want to arrive at in the course of a session of drinking, and then work out how many drinks you should have over what period of time to reach the BAC you have chosen.

'It is a pleasant accompaniment to fish, shellfish, and the lighter meats, but its delicate flavour is perhaps even more appreciated at the end of the meal with melon or dessert.'

BACs are usually recorded in milligrams of alcohol per 100 millilitres of blood. This can be shortened to milligrams per cent, written as mg%. This is the method we will use in this book. You probably know that the legal driving limit in Britain is 80mg%. The equivalent figure on the breath analyser is 35 micrograms per cent.

After drinking one unit of alcohol (e.g. one whisky or one half pint of beer), the average man is likely to reach a BAC of about 15 mg%. For the average woman, the figure is about 20 mg% (see page 17). It takes your body roughly one hour to get rid of one unit of alcohol. You can use this simple formula to calculate very roughly how long it will be before there is no alcohol left in your bloodstream.

However, the level of your BAC at any given time after drinking doesn't just depend on how much you have drunk, but on a number of other factors as well. The most important of these are as follows:

Your weight
The same amount of alcohol has a greater effect on a light person than a heavy person.

Your body composition
If they both consume the same amount of alcohol, a fat person will have a higher BAC than a lean and muscular person of the same weight.

How long you have been drinking
The same amount of alcohol knocked back quickly will result in a higher BAC than if it is drunk over a longer period. This is because you are drinking the alcohol much faster than the liver can remove it and, therefore, alcohol builds up in the bloodstream. Spacing your drinks out gives the liver a chance to burn up the alcohol at a rate which is closer to the rate you are taking it in.

Your sex
Women reach a somewhat higher BAC than men for the same amount of drink, irrespective of weight, because women have less water in their bodies.

Eating before or during drinking

As already explained, the presence of food in the stomach slows down the absorption of alcohol and therefore makes for lower BACs than drinking on an empty stomach.

How can you reach the BAC you want?

This is the vital question but, as we have seen already, this depends on a great many factors and people vary from each other considerably. We can give only a rough guide.

Instead of printing complicated tables for you to examine, we have decided to pick out a few BACs and concentrate on those. There is a special reason for choosing each of these BACs.

BAC = 50 mg %

This will give you a pleasant feeling of being 'high' without being in any way 'intoxicated'. However, your judgement may be slightly impaired and your risk of accidents will be increased.

BAC = 80 mg%

This, of course, is the legal limit for driving. But, if you aim for this BAC, this is no guarantee that you will definitely be fit to drive. However, if you drink more than the amounts given in the tables, you almost certainly *will* be over the legal limit. At this BAC, you will lose a little self-control and your reactions may be somewhat slower.

BAC = 120 mg%

You will get quite merry and you may become rather clumsy and act impulsively. You may decide that this is about as drunk as you would wish to get, even when celebrating.

Because BAC varies according to sex, weight and how long you have been drinking, we have taken these three factors into account in giving the number of drinks needed to reach a given BAC. Now consult the tables.

BAC 50 (Breath alcohol: approx. 23)

Men	One hour	Two hours	Three hours	Four hours	Five hours
9 to 11 stones	2 units	3 units	4 units	4¹/₂ units	5 units
11 to 13 stones	2¹/₂ units	4 units	5 units	5¹/₂ units	6 units
13 st or over	3 units	4¹/₂ units	5¹/₂ units	5¹/₂ units	6 units

Women	One hour	Two hours	Three hours	Four hours	Five hours
9 st or under	1¹/₂ units	2 units	2¹/₂ units	3 units	3¹/₂ units
9 to 11 stones	2 units	2¹/₂ units	3¹/₂ units	4 units	4¹/₂ units
11 st or over	2¹/₂ units	3 units	4 units	5 units	5¹/₂ units

BAC 80 (Breath alcohol: approx. 35)

Men	One hour	Two hours	Three hours	Four hours	Five hours
9 to 11 stones	3¹/₂ units	4 units	5 units	5¹/₂ units	6¹/₂ units
11 to 13 stones	4 units	5 units	6 units	6¹/₂ units	7¹/₂ units
13 st or over	5 units	6 units	7 units	7¹/₂ units	8 units

Women	One hour	Two hours	Three hours	Four hours	Five hours
9 st or under	2¹/₂ units	3 units	3¹/₂ units	3¹/₂ units	4 units
9 to 11 stones	3 units	3¹/₂ units	4¹/₂ units	4¹/₂ units	5¹/₂ units
11 st or over	3¹/₂ units	4¹/₂ units	5¹/₂ units	5¹/₂ units	6 units

BAC 120 (Breath alcohol: approx 55)

Men	One hour	Two hours	Three hours	Four hours	Five hours
9 to 11 stones	5¹/₂ units	6 units	6¹/₂ units	7 units	7¹/₂ units
11 to 13 stones	6 units	7 units	8 units	8¹/₂ units	9 units
13 st or over	7¹/₂ units	8¹/₂ units	9 units	9¹/₂ units	10 units

Women	One hour	Two hours	Three hours	Four hours	Five hours
9 st or under	3¹/₂ units	4 units	4¹/₂ units	4¹/₂ units	5 units
9 to 11 stones	4¹/₂ units	5 units	5¹/₂ units	5¹/₂ units	6 units
11 st or over	5 units	6 units	6¹/₂ units	6¹/₂ units	7 units

To help you understand how to use the BAC tables, let us consider an example. If you are a 12-stone man and wished to know what rate of drinking would make you feel pleasant without being drunk, you should refer to the first table (BAC = 50 mg%) for males. Look down the left-hand column which gives you weights and read straight across from the box with 11 to 13 stones. Your answer would therefore be 2$\frac{1}{2}$ units in one hour, or 4 units in 2 hours, or 5 units in 3 hours, or 5$\frac{1}{2}$ units in 4 hours. Having decided how long you intend to drink, you can then convert the units of alcohol into the actual quantities of the drink you usually have (remembering always that one half pint of beer equals one whisky, etc.).

How different BACs affect you

We have already given some information on this when introducing the tables for the three BACs. But here is a more complete table for the likely effects of different BACs on your feelings and behaviour.

BAC	HOW YOU FEEL	HOW YOU BEHAVE
40	Begin to feel relaxed.	Increased chance of accidents.
60	Cheerful.	Poor judgement. Decisions may be affected.
80	Feelings of warmth and well being.	Some loss of inhibitions and self control. Slow reaction time. Driving definitely worse.
120	Talkative, excited and emotional.	Uninhibited, may act on impulse.
150	Silly and confused.	Speech slurred. May be aggressive.
200	Just plain drunk.	Staggering, double vision, loss of memory.
300		Unconsciousness possible.
400		Unconsciousness likely. Death not unknown.
500		Death possible.
600		Death probable.

Again the effect of a given BAC will depend on a host of factors and, as we all know, alcohol affects different people in
very different ways at different times. Therefore, the table is
only a rough guide and applies to the average drinker on the
average occasion.

Tolerance to alcohol

We can already guess what some of you may be thinking about
the effects of various BACs and the amounts of drink needed
to reach them. You may be saying to yourself: 'These tables
are daft. It would take a lot more drink than that to make me
feel silly and befuddled'; or, 'It would take more than two and
a half pints to make me lose any of my inhibitions'.

If you are saying something like this, if you do feel the
charts and list of BAC effects greatly overestimate the intoxicating properties of alcohol, then this is because you have
become *tolerant* to alcohol. The idea of tolerance is an important one and we had better go into it in more detail.

Tolerance to a drug means that, because of your heavy use
of it, it now has a lesser effect on you than it used to.
Tolerance to alcohol is thus exactly the same kind of thing as
tolerance to heroin, when a drug addict needs an increasingly
bigger 'fix' to get a 'kick' from it. In the case of alcohol,
whereas when you first started drinking you would feel giddy
and perhaps be sick after just a few pints of beer, you may now
find that it takes twice as much for the alcohol to have an
intoxicating effect. This is why you find that the table of feelings and behaviour at various BACs on page 37 overestimates
the effects of drink — it is based on fairly inexperienced
drinkers and does not take into account the tolerance which
experienced drinkers have acquired.

Tolerance does not mean that less alcohol gets into the
bloodstream or that alcohol is less damaging. In fact, because
they are able to drink larger amounts, tolerant people's drinking is likely to be more damaging. For example, you are more
likely to experience memory blackouts if you are highly tolerant.

The vitally important point about tolerance is that it is the
first step to physical dependence on alcohol and to with-

drawal symptoms (see page 2). This is partly because tolerance allows you to drink in sufficiently large amounts for withdrawal symptoms to develop.

We don't want to exaggerate here. Most drinkers have acquired some degree of tolerance without it proving too harmful. But if you are highly tolerant, this is definitely a danger sign. So, if you find you can drink the amounts given in the table on page 36 without feeling the effects of BACs given on page 37, this probably applies to you.

Perhaps the most dangerous fallacy of all surrounding drinking is the idea that it is a good thing to be able to 'hold your liquor' and not show the effects of it – and that this is an adult thing to do. Apart from the waste of money involved in buying a drug which has little effect, all this ability proves is that you have drunk too much over the years and that you are on the way to becoming physically dependent on alcohol.

We will finish this chapter with another quiz to check how much you know about alcohol and its effects. Again, if you get any of the answers wrong, you should read the relevant section again and return to the quiz to make sure you have corrected any mistakes.

A 1. 4% 2. 11% 3. 20% 4. 40% 5. 80mg %. 6. True. Because there is less water in their bodies and the concentration of alcohol is therefore higher. Also, women tend to weigh less than men. 7. Yes/Yes/No. The only thing which makes you drunk is alcohol – in whatever form it comes. 8. 400 mg % 9. 500 mg % 10. False. Your driving gets worse after any amount of alcohol. 11. True. 12. True. 13. True. 14. False. It is people who do not get drunk easily who risk being addicted. 15. False – a dangerous fallacy.

Q-U-I-Z

Tick the box you think is correct and don't look at the answers until you have finished all the questions.

1. About how much alcohol is there in ordinary beer?	4%		11%		20%
2. About how much alcohol is there in wine?	4%		11%		20%
3. About how much alcohol is there in sherry?	20%		40%		70%
4. About how much alcohol is there in gin?	20%		40%		70%
5. Which BAC is the legal driving limit in Britain?	50 mg %		80 mg %		70 mg %
6. Women get drunk more easily than men?	TRUE			FALSE	
7. Which of the following things affects how quickly you get drunk? Your weight	NO			YES	
When you last ate	NO			YES	
Mixing your drinks	NO			YES	
8. At which BAC would most people pass out?	200 mg %		300 mg %		400 mg %
9. At which BAC is it possible to die?	300 mg %		400 mg %		500 mg %
10. At a BAC of 80 mg % most people's driving begins to get worse .	TRUE			FALSE	
11. A BAC of 50 mg % would give most people a nice 'high'.	TRUE			FALSE	
12. A BAC of 120 mg % would make most people clumsy and uninhibited.	TRUE			FALSE	
13. For most people, a BAC of 200 mg % results in staggering, double-vision and loss of memory.	TRUE			FALSE	
14. People who get drunk easily are more likely to become addicted to alcohol.	TRUE			FALSE	
15. The ability to hold your drink is a good thing	TRUE			FALSE	

40

4
ALCOHOL AND YOUR HEALTH

Before reading this chapter, answer the quiz. As before, check to see whether your answers are correct after you have read the chapter.

Q-U-I-Z

1. Alcohol provides some
   important dietary requirements .... TRUE   FALSE

2. Low-sugar diet beers are much less
   fattening than other beers .... TRUE   FALSE

3. Drinking is good for the heart .... TRUE   FALSE

4. The effects of alcohol on the brain
   are only temporary .... TRUE   FALSE

5. Alcohol is a great stress reducer .... TRUE   FALSE

6. Alcohol can cause poor sleep .... TRUE   FALSE

7. The only decent way to deal with a
   hangover is by the 'hair of the dog' .... TRUE   FALSE

8. Alcohol is okay taken with safe
   tranquillizers .... TRUE   FALSE

A

1. *False.* Alcohol can actually prevent absorption of important vitamins. Alcohol only supplies fattening calories.
2. *False.* It all depends upon how much alcohol is in them; generally, the less sugar there is, the more alcohol has been fermented out of the sugar, and alcohol is very fattening.
3. *True.* But only in small amounts (1 or 2 drinks a day) and mainly in middle-aged people. Heavier drinking can cause fatal heart disease and, with some diseases, any drinking can cause harm.
4. *False.* Very heavy drinking can produce irreversible mental impairment, especially in the over 40s.
5. *False.* While in the short-term alcohol may soothe nerves, in the long-term, using alcohol as a tranquilliser produces more anxiety and stress.
6. *True.* Alcohol may get you off to sleep more quickly, but large quantities produce a poor and disturbed sleep.
7. *False.* This can be very dangerous: rest, nourishment and time are the best hangover cures.
8. *False.* There is no such thing as a 'safe' tranquilliser. Alcohol can be very dangerous taken together with tranquillizers and many other types of drug.

42

One in every five men in acute general hospital wards is a problem drinker. This figure speaks volumes about the potential impact of alcohol on a person's health. However, it is not just the problem drinker whose health is at risk – excessive drinking can seriously damage the health of most people. And for some, even moderate drinking can be harmful. So who should be careful about even moderate drinking?

- People who have suffered, or are suffering, from liver disease.

- Those with chronic stomach/intestinal problems, such as ulcers or pancreatitis.

- Diabetics and those with a family history of diabetes.

- People with some types of kidney disorder.

- People taking other drugs. (Consult your doctor about your drugs.)

- People who are abstaining following an alcohol problem.

- Pregnant women, or women thinking of becoming pregnant. (We will discuss this in more detail in the next chapter.)

REMEMBER:
IF IN DOUBT, CONSULT YOUR FAMILY DOCTOR.

And now for the good news!

Statistically speaking, moderate drinkers are a better life insurance risk than abstainers. There is evidence that moderate drinking reduces the likelihood of a first heart attack in middle-aged men and post-menopausal women. And, remember, moderate drinking means only 1 or 2 drinks a day; daily amounts over this increase the risk of illness. Used properly, alcohol can be a delightful and relaxing beverage and so, perhaps, we should not be too surprised if it has benefits for the health of many people. (But remember, heavy drinkers are a far, far worse insurance risk and what was said about the better insurance risk of moderate drinkers obviously does not apply to people who should be careful about any drinking, like those mentioned earlier.)

As described in the last chapter, alcohol is rapidly sent to almost every part of the body very soon after you take a drink. It should not be surprising, then, to discover that excessive alcohol can cause damage to many different parts of the body, ranging from the liver to the brain, and from the nose to the toes. The illustration shows just some of the danger spots for the excessive drinker.

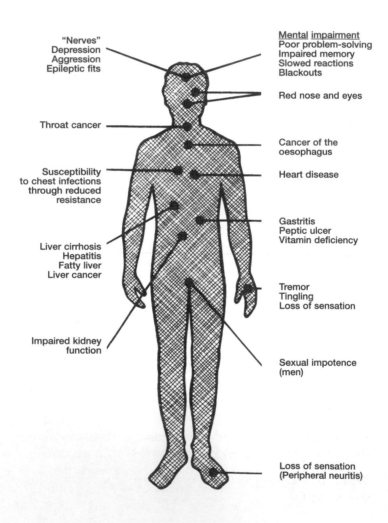

Before we make a tour round the body outlining the possible health problems alcohol can cause, let us discuss one major health issue which concerns almost everyone, and which is closely related to alcohol use.

Alcohol, weight and diet

One gin and tonic contains approximately 140 calories–roughly the same as a large ice-cream – while one pint of beer has twice as many calories as this. Do not be deceived by those low-sugar diet beers – the fact that they have less sugar usually means they have more alcohol, and alcohol is rich in calories, just like sugar.

© Barry Fantoni   *"Slimline tonic!"*

So does drinking make you fat? Well, it can, but excessive drinking can also lead to malnutrition. How can this be? The answer is complicated but goes something like this:

＊ Ordinary calories which are not burned up by the body are stored in the liver as glycogen.

＊ When the body needs more energy, it converts some of this glycogen back into energy-providing glucose.

＊ When the glycogen store is full up, the extra calories are stored as fat.

* Here is the catch. The liver cannot store up calories which come from alcohol: it can only burn them up immediately.

* This means that alcohol calories push aside food calories, so that these get stored as glycogen and then fat.

* So, it isn't the alcohol which makes you fat; rather, it's the food which the liver does not have time to burn up because it is too busy dealing with the alcohol.

* Alcohol is a very efficient producer of calories, but it does not supply vitamins, proteins or other necessary nutrients.

* Thus heavy drinkers can develop a beer belly and be under-nourished at the same time.

For this reason, many heavy drinkers – especially beer drinkers – become fat, although this is not true for all of them. Many drinkers lose their appetite after several drinks, and many excessive drinkers eat very little while drinking. So some heavy drinkers become very thin.

As is so often the case with alcohol, however, a little alcohol can have very different effects from a lot – small amounts of alcohol stimulate the gastric juices and serve as appetizers. Thus alcohol's effects on weight and nutrition are complicated. So, please do not console yourself with the thought that you are either too fat or too thin to be drinking too much: excessive drinking can make you fat or thin, depending upon your own circumstances. But moderate amounts of alcohol can make you enjoy food even more.

Count up how many calories of alcohol you have drunk in the past week and note them in the table on page 48. To help you, here is a list of drinks with their equivalent calorie content.

DRINK	CALORIES
1 pint of beer	300
1 glass of wine	80
1 gin and tonic	140
1 whisky	90
1 vodka and orange	130

■ Remember: 10000 extra calories will produce 3 pounds of fat.

■ This means that $2^{1}/_{2}$ pints of beer a day for 2 weeks could put on 3 pounds of weight.

■ Two gins and tonic a day for 5 weeks could fatten you by 3 pounds.

One final note on diet

Alcohol can stop your body absorbing vitamins even if you are eating well. The B-vitamins are especially vulnerable and, among some very heavy drinkers, severe brain damage can be caused by a deficiency in thiamine – Vitamin B1 – because the alcohol stops it being absorbed. Wernicke-Korsakoff's syndrome leads to the sufferers not being able to remember new information: they forget where they are, what year it is, and cannot remember faces or names. Even after months in a hospital ward, they still cannot find the way to the toilet.

Calorie Diary
FOR THE LAST SEVEN DAYS

Day	Drinks	Calories
1		
2		
3		
4		
5		
6		
7		
	TOTAL	

This dramatic example may apply only to a minority of very heavy drinkers, yet a high proportion of heavy drinkers may be suffering ill health because their bodies are not absorbing important vitamins – especially vitamins B and C. There is some evidence to suggest that among very heavy drinkers, those who are poorly nourished are more likely to be mentally impaired by alcohol, even when they have not drunk for a week or two. This brings us to the first stop on our tour of the alcohol-affected body – the brain.

Alcohol and the brain

It is precisely because of its effects on the brain that human beings have taken so eagerly to alcohol for millennia. Of course, we enjoy its taste and for some connoisseurs of wine or malt whisky, for instance, the taste is all important. Yet even one drink has an effect on the brain, and most drinkers enjoy this. We already mentioned in Chapter 3 how alcohol has a depressant effect on the central nervous system: 'messages' take longer to travel along the nerves in the brain under the influence of the drug, and hence reaction times are slowed, thinking becomes quirky and sluggish and co-ordination suffers. Complex mental tasks are the most vulnerable to the effects of alcohol and, in particular, activities which require us to divide our attention between two or more tasks.

Driving a car is a good example of this. While we are driving, we must keep track of what is happening on the road, check the mirror regularly, change gear, watch for traffic signals, etc. Alcohol acts like a spanner in the works of this complex activity; hence the hundreds of thousands of people who have died or been maimed because of alcohol-impaired driving.

What has this to do with health? Apart from the obvious issue of alcohol-related accidents, it appears to be the case that, with repeated heavy drinking, the effects of alcohol begin to last longer and longer after drinking stops. In people under the age of about 40, while this mental impairment can last for months after heavy drinking ceases, much of it is recoverable – the impairment is not permanent.

However, for the over-40s, it seems that the dulling effects of alcohol on mental acuteness are much less easily reversible, and in some cases are *irreversible*. It seems as if the older brain can become like an old worn rubber band which has been stretched once too often, thus losing its elasticity. Seldom is this loss of mental ability obvious to friends and family, as vocabulary and conversation are usually not noticeably affected. It is more abstract activities, such as problem solving, which are more likely to be impaired. Thus, it may be that a person's workmates notice problems in this area before friends and family do, assuming the drinker works in an intellectually demanding job.

Some very heavy, habitual drinkers also suffer from 'delirium tremens' – a quite dangerous state of alcohol withdrawal which causes violent tremors, hallucinations, disorientation, rambling speech and hyperactivity and which usually takes place three to four days after very heavy drinking has stopped. Between 15 and 30 per cent of people in the 'DTs' die, though there are several less severe levels of withdrawal which come on sooner after heavy drinking stops. Some heavy drinkers can also suffer alcohol-induced epileptic-type fits, and heavy drinkers also tend to be prone to head injuries, which can affect their mental capacities even more.

Alcohol and the liver

As numerous elixir-flogging quacks through the centuries will testify, the liver is an extremely important bodily organ. It carries out the tough job of converting what we eat and drink into useable nutrition, while discreetly disposing of the noxious substances which do us no good at all. Alcohol is a poisonous substance, and the liver is the only organ capable of neutralizing it. It does this by producing an enzyme called ADH (alcohol dehydrogenase) whose only function in life is to change alcohol to acetaldehyde. (Quite why humans possess an enzyme whose only purpose is to attack alcohol is a puzzle.) This acetaldehyde is, however, even more poisonous than alcohol, and is quickly changed to acetic acid – in other words, vinegar. The vinegar then burns up to water and carbon dioxide and thence to the calories which give us our day-to-day energy.

But, as is the case with the reprocessing of nuclear waste, things are not as easy as all this – large and frequent chemical reactions produce regular 'fall-out', and this can be harmful. So, even though the acetaldehyde is only around for a short time before it is turned to vinegar, if this happens often enough and in large enough quantities, it can do harm. One type of harm is to interfere with the absorption of some of the B-vitamins.

Apart from this, many other complex chemical side-effects of working the liver too hard can take place. Three main types of liver damage can result: alcoholic cirrhosis, alcoholic hepatitis and alcoholic fatty liver. The first of these, cirrhosis, is a very serious medical condition which kills about 10 per cent of people who have been serious problem drinkers for 10 years or more. Alcoholic hepatitis leads on to cirrhosis in about 50 per cent of cases, but is not quite so serious as cirrhosis. A fatty liver is generally reversible with a nutritious diet and abstinence from alcohol.

'I bet whoever gets your liver won't wake up bright and smiling!'

© 1982, Osbert Lancaster.

Alcohol and the heart

As we have just noted, the very heavy drinker tends to build up deposits of fat on the liver. The liver is, however, a very sturdy organ which can 'shake off' some of this fat into the bloodstream. Some of the extra fat in the blood may collect around the heart and increase the risk of heart disease.

As mentioned earlier in the chapter, there is now good evidence that light drinking is linked with a lower risk for certain types of heart disease; in other words, compared with total abstention from alcohol, light drinking has a 'protective effect' against coronary heart disease. Although the way this protective effect is caused is not definitely known, it is thought that alcohol raises levels of a special kind of protein in the blood known as 'high density lipoproteins'. This helps to prevent the formation of deposits of fatty tissues in the arteries that are the major cause of heart attacks. Alcohol may also help to prevent coronary heart disease in other ways but these are more speculative at present. And remember that the protective effect of alcohol applies only to groups who are at significant risk of heart disease in the first place – i.e., middle-aged men and women mainly in western, industralized countries. Lastly, always bear in mind that the protective effect applies only at low levels of alcohol consumption of around 1 or 2 units per day. If drinking increases much over this, the protective effect is overtaken by increasing risk of getting other diseases.

Another possible misunderstanding of the evidence on the protective effect of alcohol would be to conclude that people who are abstinent should be advised to take up drinking. This is not the case. There are other ways of preventing heart disease than by drinking, e.g. taking an aspirin every other day, eating a healthy diet and regularly engaging in healthy exercise. And the evidence shows that encouraging more people to become drinkers would increase the total harm caused by alcohol in the population at large. Also, of course, if someone's non-drinking means they have had an alcohol problem in the past, they are far better off sticking to abstinence and avoiding the perils of returning to drinking.

Alcohol and stress

As we said in the last chapter, alcohol is a depressant drug. Because of this, it acts as a tranquillizer for people who are very anxious. So does this mean that alcohol reduces stress? Well, it may do so for moderate drinkers, but once you start drinking above the levels which we recommended in Chapter 2 (i.e., 21 units per week for men, 14 units per week for women), then **alcohol can increase stress.**

Why is this? When the nervous system is 'weighed down' by a drug – tranquillizers, sleeping tablets, heroin, alcohol, etc. – then once the drug is removed, the nervous system 'rebounds' like a coiled spring which is released. The opposite effects to those of the drug then appear – tension, nervousness, restlessness – and may remain for hours, days or even weeks. In the case of some drugs, such as the benzodiazepines, some people suffer these withdrawal symptoms for months or even years.

If you drink regularly and heavily – say four pints per day if you are male, or four vodkas per day if you are female – then your nervous system is 'weighed down' by the alcohol. If you miss drinking for a day or two, you may well experience 'rebound' symptoms similar to those described above, i.e. you may feel nervy and stressed. These feelings can also creep up on you even though you keep on drinking, because your body becomes tolerant to the effects of alcohol. Also, you may be emotionally depressed because of the physiological effects of the drug.

The biggest problem with these effects of alcohol is in recognizing them for what they are. People are often not aware that they are feeling this way until they stop or cut down their drinking. And if they are aware of the feelings, too often they try to overcome them by – yes, you've guessed it – more alcohol. Some old-fashioned family doctors have done untold harm by advising jaded housewives to 'take a drink of sherry' when they are feeling low. Some of these housewives are feeling low precisely because of drinking. And for those who are not, they may have been encouraged on a damaging career of drinking as a form of self-medication. We know that drinking for this reason leads all too often to disastrous consequences. We will discuss this issue in more detail in Chapters 6 and 8.

Alcohol and sleep

Alcohol has short-term positive effects – for instance, it reduces anxiety – yet in the long term it can cause increases in anxiety and depression. Exactly the same applies for sleep. Of course, a small nightcap is relatively harmless and is probably preferable to long-term use of sleeping pills. However, large doses of alcohol get you off to sleep quickly, but tend to lead to poorer sleep.

One reason for this is that alcohol supresses one particular type of sleep, known as REM sleep. REM stands for 'rapid eye movement' and, in this stage of sleep, our eyes tend to flicker and move. This is when we dream. Thus, alcohol reduces the 'dream sleep' which is a necessary part of our night's rest and, if we are deprived of it, we tend to feel tired and unrested. If we stop drinking for a day or two, the brain tends to 'rebound' and make up for lost dreams by increasing REM sleep. This tends to lead to bad dreams, nightmares and restless sleep. (This process also happens with many tranquillizers and sleeping pills.)

Alcohol and other drugs

Many people who drink too much also take other drugs, such as tranquillizers, anti-depressants and sleeping pills, not to mention painkillers, stomach preparations and many more. This is because heavy drinkers suffer a lot of physical and psychological ill health. Many try to treat the symptoms of excessive drinking with other mood-altering drugs. This never works in the long term and can lead to terrible problems.

Why is this? One reason is simply that alcohol and some other drugs can interact to produce an effect which is far greater than the sum of each of the individual effects. Therefore 'safe' amounts of alcohol taken with 'safe' amounts of some other drug can together be lethal. For no drug is this more true than barbiturates, commonly used in the treatment of epilepsy. One or two barbiturate tablets taken with three or four drinks can kill you, yet in the past barbiturates were widely prescribed as sleeping pills!

There is also evidence that alcohol and tranquillizers can show cross-tolerance. That is, if you become tolerant to one, this tolerance can carry over to the other. So, for instance, if you have been on a tranquillizer for several months so that it no longer has the same effect as before, and you then begin to drink, the alcohol may not have much of an effect until you have several drinks. This is obviously dangerous, because it means you will tend to take more of both drugs to achieve the effects they had at first. Thus dependence on one drug can 'spread' to another.

'Stimulant' drugs, such as the caffeine found in coffee and tea, are sometimes taken to try to counteract the effects of alcohol. The 'black coffee cure' is a myth, as we said in the last chapter. Large amounts of stimulant drugs taken with alcohol can place great strain on the cardiovascular system, and amphetamines are the worst offenders here. So beware of 'diet drugs' which contain stimulants: the combination of these with alcohol may put an excessive strain on your heart.

Many other drugs may interact with alcohol. Some antidepressants, for instance, seem to exaggerate the depressive effects of alcohol on the central nervous system, much in the way that barbiturates do. Antihistamines can make you drowsy and, taken with alcohol, this effect may be increased. Car driving and the operation of machinery may suffer and you run the risk of injury in an accident. This, of course, applies to many of the drugs which we have mentioned. If taken with alcohol, some painkillers – including aspirin – can result in a worsening of various stomach problems. And alcohol tends to reduce the absorption of antibiotics and hence makes them somewhat less effective.

The message is clear, then: alcohol is a drug, and when more than one drug is taken, problems can occur. So beware of taking alcohol with other drugs and, if in any doubt, consult your doctor.

Some other effects of alcohol

When we feel a warm glow after drinking, this is a sign that many of the cells of our bodies are bathed in ethyl alcohol. If this happens often enough and with sufficient quantities of alcohol, then changes can take place in some cells. At times these changes can be malignant. For instance, problem drinkers are at higher than average risk for cancers of the throat and liver.

Stomach disorders such as gastritis are also common. Gastritis is a result of alcohol stripping parts of the stomach of its mucous lining, which leads to pain and diarrhoea. In extreme cases this can lead to prolonged vomiting and bleeding. Peptic ulcers are also a common consequence of prolonged heavy drinking.

There are many other diseases which are caused by heavy drinking. One reason for this link is that large quantities of alcohol suppress the immune system – the body's own defence against disease and injury. This, taken with the vitamin deficiencies which are common in heavy drinkers, leaves them vulnerable to all sorts of disease.

Alcohol also has the effect of stimulating insulin production in the pancreas. Insulin reduces sugar levels in the blood and can lead to hypoglycaemia, or low blood-sugar. Low blood-sugar produces feelings of drowsiness, weakness, trembling, faintness and hunger. Some of the hangover effects of alcohol are caused by this. Large doses of sugar can also stimulate the body to produce insulin and, because of this, can result in even lower blood-sugar levels. So if alcohol and sugar are taken together, especially where blood-sugar levels are already low, a big insulin reaction can be the result, followed by a hypoglycaemic reaction. This only happens to some people, however, but if you are one of them, beware of gins and tonic or whiskies and ginger ale on an empty stomach! And if you are diabetic, take extra care because alcohol may seriously de-stabilize your insulin–sugar balance.

Finally, what about alcohol and sex? The real physiological effects of alcohol are to reduce sexual functioning somewhat, both in men (decreased penile tumescence) and in women (decreased vaginal lubrication). However, through films, television and advertisements, Western society does its best to persuade drinkers that alcohol is an aphrodisiac and a key to sexual adventure. And if we believe that, then we will act as if it were true. Research has shown that the sexually stimulating effects of alcohol are caused by believing that you have drunk alcohol, not whether you actually have drunk it. Thus, in some ways, alcohol is a 'ticket' to behave in ways in which we would not otherwise allow ourselves.

However, as with almost all the effects of alcohol, too much does lead to serious problems. Impotence in men who are problem drinkers is not uncommon, and this can happen for a mixture of physical and psychological reasons. We will discuss some sexual problems related to alcohol in more detail in Chapter 8.

Another sexual issue that has caused some concern, particularly in relation to youngsters, is the danger that alcohol intoxication leads people to engage in unsafe sex and thereby increases the risk of contracting or spreading HIV – the virus that causes AIDS. There has been a lot of research on this topic and, on the whole, findings do not bear out the more alarmist views of some commentators. It may be true that heavier drinkers are more likely to engage in high risk sex than lighter drinkers but it has not definitely been shown that people are less likely to use condoms after drinking. Nevertheless, health education about HIV and AIDS should be directed at all sexually-active people and education about sex, alcohol and drugs should begin at an early age.

This chapter has concentrated more on alcohol and disease than upon alcohol and health. This is because most people are simply not aware of the potential dangers of heavy drinking. Perhaps the greatest health hazard of all is from accidents – on the road, at work and in the house. Thousands of people in Britain are killed, and tens of thousands more maimed by themselves or by others because of drinking too much. In later chapters of the book, we turn to a discussion of why you may be drinking more than is good for you, and what you can do about it.

5
WOMEN AND ALCOHOL

The first question you may be asking here is, why devote a separate chapter to women? After all, women are members of the human race. Why should they be singled out in this way and why isn't there also a chapter called 'Men and Alcohol'? In fact, there are three reasons for paying special attention to women in this book, but before going into them, try the quiz to see how much you already know about women and alcohol.

Q-U-I-Z

1. The drinking problems of women are insignificant compared with those of men.	TRUE	FALSE
2. Generally speaking, women get drunk on less alcohol than men.	TRUE	FALSE
3. This is because: a) women usually weigh less than men.	TRUE	FALSE
b) women have less water in their bodies than men.	TRUE	FALSE
c) women absorb more alcohol into the bloodstream than men.	TRUE	FALSE
4. Female heavy drinkers are more likely to develop liver disease than male heavy drinkers.	TRUE	FALSE
5. Female heavy drinkers are more at risk for becoming dependent on alcohol.	TRUE	FALSE
6. Female heavy drinkers are more likely to suffer from depression.	TRUE	FALSE
7. In pregnancy, it is only alcoholics who risk damage to the baby.	TRUE	FALSE
8. The best advice for pregnant women is to cut down to one or two units of alcohol once or twice a week or else abstain completely during pregnancy.	TRUE	FALSE

A

1.False – and female drinking problems are increasing **2.** Unfortunate but true. **3a.** True. **3b.** True. **3c.** True. **4.** True – for reasons which are not fully understood. **5.** True. **6.** True. **7.** False – damage can occur at lower levels of drinking than shown by alcoholics. **8.** True – at the present state of our knowledge.

59

The reasons for devoting a special chapter to women and alcohol are as follow:

First, until quite recently women tended to be ignored in books written about alcohol and its problems. It was simply assumed that drinking alcohol was mainly a masculine thing to do and that whatever problems alcohol caused were largely confined to men. Over the last 10 years there has been an increasing awareness of female drinking and related problems, and a large amount of research in this area. This new attention to women's drinking is fully justified as a correction to the previous neglect of the subject and we shall follow suit here.

Second, we said earlier (page 8) that drinking problems have been increasing in Britain and other parts of the world over the last 40 to 50 years. But the point is that the drinking problems of women have been increasing at a higher rate than the average – higher than for men. It is estimated that, 20 years ago, for every women requesting help for a drinking problem, there were eight men. Now that figure is down to one woman for every two men. As this shows, men are still more likely to seek help for a problem, but women are catching up fast! It may also be true that more women are coming forward for help because they feel less ashamed of their problem than they used to. Let us hope so. But, even so, there has undoubtedly been a real and dramatic increase in the number of women experiencing problems with their drinking in recent times.

The *third* reason for singling out women is that they have special problems connected with their drinking. In the first place, women are more at risk for being harmed by alcohol than men. You must have noticed, especially if you are a female reader, that the recommended weekly alcohol level for women on page 17 is lower than the one for men – quite a bit lower! This may seem terribly unfair on women, but the fact is that it takes less alcohol to cause problems in women than it does in men. We will go into the reasons for this shortly.

As well as being at greater risk, there are problems applying to women which obviously do not affect men at all – problems connected with menstruation, the menopause, pregnancy, breast feeding and the contraceptive pill. We will deal with each of these 'special problems' in this chapter, but first let us try to prove that advising women to drink less than men is not just a sexist plot to stop them enjoying themselves.

Why women should drink less than men

Women have much greater social freedom (including the freedom to drink) than they used to, say 20 or 30 years ago. This is undoubtedly a good thing but it also has its negative side because some women may imagine that they can drink as much as men. They may attempt to keep up with the drinking rates of their male partners. The problem is that, for unavoidable biological reasons, this is not a good idea.

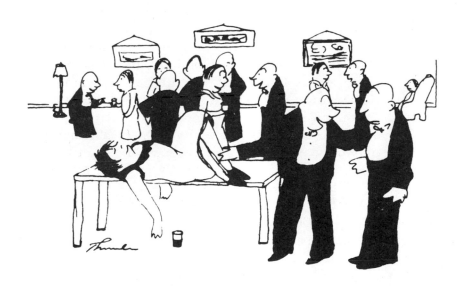

"And this is the little woman."

It is an unfortunate but unavoidable fact that women get drunk more easily than men. The reasons for this are quite straightforward. In the first place, women tend to weigh less than men; the average body weight for women is 60kg (9st. 8lb) compared with 70kg (11 st.) for men. This means that a given amount of alcohol will result in a higher Blood Alcohol Concentration (see page 32) in the average woman compared with the average man.

Added to that, women, especially young women, have a lower proportion of their total body weight in the form of water; for men it is about 60 per cent but for women 50 per cent. The consequence is that the same number of drinks produces a higher concentration of alcohol in the blood. We also know that, in women, more of the alcohol they drink gets into the bloodstream, so that the peak BAC is reached sooner after having a drink than in men. Thus, not only do women reach a higher BAC for the same amount of drink, but they reach it sooner than do men. The opposite of this is that women eliminate alcohol faster than men – their alcohol metabolism is more efficient. So, although women get drunk more quickly, they sober up more quickly too.

Nevertheless, when calculating how much they should drink to reach the BAC they have chosen (see pages 32–38), women should use different figures from men. This is why we presented the BAC conversion tables on page 36 separately for the two sexes. A convenient rule of thumb is that, at an average rate of drinking, one standard unit of alcohol will produce a BAC of 15 mg% in men but 20 mg% in women. For example, to reach a BAC of 60 mg%, a woman should drink three units (3 glasses of spirits or 1½ pints of beer) in two hours.

More bad news for women!

The other main reason for advising women to drink less than men is that they are more liable to damage their health through excessive drinking. The most obvious example of this is liver disease. Women have a greater chance of contracting liver disease than men drinking the same amount; women get liver cirrhosis after a shorter history of heavy drinking and as a result of lower average quantities of alcohol drunk; and if they do suffer from liver damage, women are more likely to develop serious forms of the disease (e.g., to progress from alcoholic hepatitis to liver cirrhosis) and more likely to die from it.

Exactly why women are at greater risk from liver disease is not known for certain. It may be because of the way women drink compared to men – more regular excessive drinking as opposed to occasional heavy binges – but this is probably not the full story. Because, as we have seen, more alcohol is taken up into the bloodstream in women, the liver has more work to do and this may be a factor in their greater risk of liver damage. Differences in the immune systems of men and women have also been suggested, but there is no firm evidence as yet.

Nor is liver disease the only kind of illness which female problem drinkers are more likely to get. There is some evidence to suggest that women in this group are more likely to suffer from depression, to use other drugs (including tobacco) and are at greater risk from brain damage, certain cancers of the head and neck, and ulcers. What we can be certain of is that the death rate in female excessive drinkers is significantly higher than in men. Everybody who drinks too much is risking shortening their life-span but, for women, these risks are even greater than for their male counterparts.

Quite apart from risks of contracting diseases related to drinking, women are also more likely than men to become dependent on alcohol. Thus, women tend to show signs of physical dependence (e.g., withdrawal symptoms) earlier on in their drinking history and at lower levels of alcohol consumption. The reasons for this are again not fully understood, but it partly accounts for the fact that women attending treatment centres for alcoholism are found to have been drinking heavily for fewer years than their male fellow-patients .

But it is not all bad news for women. It seems that women heavy drinkers may be less likely to develop certain kinds of heart disease than male heavy drinkers. Also, men can suffer from shrinkage of the testicles and excessive drinking can lead to a low sperm count, making male problem drinkers less fertile.

Drinking and the menstrual cycle

It is thought that female psychology and behaviour may be affected in many ways both positive and negative by the menstrual cycle. Women experiencing premenstrual tension (PMT) can vary from feeling slightly irritable to being severely depressed. A short-lived depression after childbirth is fairly common and later the menopause brings psychological changes, including problems, for many women. These are both partly consequences of changes in hormone levels.

It is commonly believed that female drinking and its effects are related to the menstrual cycle. However, the latest evidence suggests that it is difficult to be sure how one thing affects the other. There is even some more recent work to suggest that sex hormone fluctuations in women may not be as important in affecting alcohol metabolism as testerone levels in men. So generalizations about alcohol effects and the menstrual cycle are hazardous.

The same applies to the effects of alcohol and the contraceptive pill. Some older research studies which found that taking the pill made BACs more regular have now been questioned. The only thing it is fairly safe to conclude is that, owing to a range of complex factors, the effects of alcohol and BACs reached vary more in women than in men. This obviously increases the danger of drinking and driving in women. As we said before (p. 20), the safest policy is not to drink at all before driving.

There has also been a lot of speculation about the role of PMT in the causes of drinking problems among women. It is undoubtedly true that some women drink to ease the symptoms of PMT. This need not necessarily become a problem, although it is not generally a good idea to drink alcohol regularly to get relief from anxiety or depression (see page 105). There has also been a suggestion that many women with drinking problems increase their intake during the premenstrual phase, and women who are trying to abstain from alcohol or to cut down to safer levels may find it difficult not to relapse just before their period.

Alcohol and pregnancy

In 1981, the Surgeon General of the United States of America made an official statement to all women who were pregnant, or who were thinking about becoming pregnant, advising them to abstain totally from alcohol. Some people think that a similar warning should be given in Britain.

The possibility that drinking by pregnant women can harm the health of their future offspring has been known for a very long time. There are references to it in the Old Testament and it was known to the Greek philosopher, Aristotle. In recent times, however, doctors have paid much more attention to this possibility following the discovery of something called the Fetal Alcohol Syndrome (or FAS for short) in the babies of alcoholic women. At first, British doctors were much more cautious about this syndrome than their colleagues in America and Europe, but most would now agree that the FAS definitely does exist.

Part of the problem is that the FAS is difficult to recognize, because its symptoms are similar to those produced by smoking, poor nutrition and other drug use. Social deprivation is also a major factor linked with the FAS. But when all the features of the syndrome are present, the FAS forms a unique pattern of physical and mental handicap, with below average weight and height, typical facial features and damage to other organs of the body. Sadly, children born with this syndrome never catch up with other children in any of these areas.

The Fetal Alcohol Syndrome is a very abnormal and tragic condition, and it usually only occurs in the babies of women who could be labelled as 'alcoholics' or 'problem drinkers'. *But it is important to understand that the harm caused by drinking during pregnancy may not be just a question of the full FAS.* There is a lot of research to suggest that drinking below 'alcoholic' levels – even moderate drinking – can have harmful effects on the fetus. It is true that the meaning of these findings is still being hotly debated; some experts believe that other factors – especially poor diet, smoking, illegal drug use and other things linked with social deprivation – have more power to damage the fetus than moderate levels of drinking.

And, of course, it is not claimed that the harmful effects of alcohol always occur – once again, it is a matter of risks. But when they do happen, they seem to be a less pronounced version of the FAS, including poor birth weight and lowered IQ. Rather than a Fetal Alcohol Syndrome, we are concerned here with 'fetal alcohol effects'.

The question of how much alcohol a pregnant woman can drink without harming her baby is one which has produced a stormy debate among doctors. It has been one of the most controversial topics in medical circles in recent years and all sorts of accusations have been made by one side or the other. Some doctors say no alcohol at all should be drunk during pregnancy, but other think that small amounts do no harm and that to advise against drinking completely will just cause unnecessary alarm to women. Experts in Britain tend to be less extreme on this issue than those in the USA where pregnant women are usually advised to abstain totally. In the UK, the most common and consistent advice is that *one or two units of alcohol once or twice a week* has not been shown to be harmful.

Needless to say, if a pregnant woman chooses to give up alcohol altogether, no-one should try to persuade her otherwise. Some women might think that, in a situation where only a few drinks per week are allowed, one might as well not bother with alcohol.

There is also the question of when in pregnancy the damage is done. With the FAS, it is more likely that it occurs very early in pregnancy, when the nervous system is rapidly developing. This is why women are best advised to cut out drinking or reduce it to very low levels even if they are just considering getting pregnant – the harm may be done before they even realize they have conceived.

Unfortunately, we know that saying things like this may cause alarm to women who discover they are pregnant and remember that they must have been drinking after conception. What must be borne in mind is that, once again, it is all a question of risks. The fact that you have been drinking before you realized that you were pregnant does not at all mean that your baby is *bound* to have been damaged. So there is no need to panic. Indeed, if the amounts you drank were moderate, the chances of damage are very low.

All this does not mean that the early months are the only time when harm may be caused. Heavy drinking during the second and third trimesters (i.e., three month periods) harms the growth of the baby's body and brain. And even if a woman has been drinking heavily in early pregnancy, it is still worth cutting down or giving up later on. This is because the babies of lighter drinkers tend to be bigger and this gives them a better chance of survival. So there is always something that can be done to help the baby

Luckily, nature seems to have found its own safety mechanism for dealing with the potential harm of alcohol during pregnancy – the fact that many women develop an aversion to alcohol, as well as being put off other possibly harmful substances, like coffee and cigarettes. Unfortunately, if someone has become dependent on alcohol, this is less likely to happen and even if drinking is reduced, it may still continue at harmful levels. This is why pregnant women who are dependent on alcohol need special help. If you are in this situation, visit your doctor or use the list of addresses at the end of this book.

On a related subject, the possible harm caused by drinking does not end when the baby has been born; it also applies to breast-feeding. In the same way that alcohol passes through the placenta into the blood circulation of the fetus, so it passes into the mother's milk. The concentration of alcohol in the milk will be about the same as the mother's BAC and the effects of large doses on the baby may be serious. What is more, the passage of milk to the baby may be impaired by alcohol, making feeding more difficult. Contrary to popular belief, if a woman is having difficulty breast feeding her baby, it is not a good idea to drink alcohol before feeding. Alcohol may actually make the milk taste bitter and, if the baby is not feeding well, this obviously will not help the situation. So, if you do have a couple of drinks, make sure there is enough time for the alcohol to be eliminated from the body (see pages 28–29) before breast feeding begins.

The danger from drug cocktails

In the previous chapter, we discussed the dangers of mixing alcohol with other drugs. The reason for mentioning the topic again in this chapter is that women are especially vulnerable to the harm caused by 'drug cocktails'. In total, women take about twice as many mood-altering drugs as men and, for many women, this is their main way of trying to cope with the stresses and strains of life.

So, the simple advice is: if you are being prescribed any of the drugs mentioned in Chapter 4 by your doctor, you should not drink alcohol. If in doubt, ask your doctor whether it is safe to drink or not.

Warnings for the weight conscious

Women are also likely to be more concerned about their weight than men. This is because our kind of society puts a lot of pressure on women to be slim and attractive.

Be that as it may, if you are someone who is particularly anxious to avoid putting on weight, you should be aware that alcohol is packed with calories. If taken in excess, alcohol is very fattening. Some lagers are advertised as being low in sugar, but the snag here is that this also means that they are stronger than normal. So return to the last chapter and decide whether your use of alcohol is contributing to a weight problem.

Why are women drinking more than they used to?

Underlying the figures about the rise in female drinking problems given at the start of the chapter is the fact that womens' consumption of alcohol has gone up enormously over the last fifty years. More women are drinking and those who do drink are drinking more than they used to. Why is this?

One obvious set of factors has to do with the changing position of women in society and in the family over the years in question.

* **First,** many more women are in work than previously and the earnings of working women have gone up more in comparison with the earnings of men (although they still earn less than men in many cases). Thus, women have more money to spend on drink than they used to. Added to this, many women are waiting longer to start their families and so have a longer period of time with good earning power and relatively few responsibilities.

* **Second,** although we told you before that all alcohol has become cheaper in real terms over the years, the drinks favoured by many women – gin, white rum, sherry, liqueurs and all kinds of wine – have gone down in real terms even more than mens' favourite drink, beer. It is true that many young women these days like beer, lager and exotic 'designer drinks' but on the whole, the drinks women prefer are cheaper to buy. It is also much easier for women to purchase alcohol to drink at home since it became available in supermarkets.

* **Third,** just as important as these economic reasons, it is now far more acceptable for women to drink than it used to be. Thirty years ago, women drinking in pubs, if not accompanied by their husbands or boyfriends, were frowned on and could even be suspected of being there for immoral purposes. Now, of course, it is quite normal for a group of women friends to visit a pub. Generally speaking, the stigma attached to womens' drinking has largely disappeared and it is now a fashionable activity, especially for young women.

Of course, these trends have been noticed by the advertisers. You must have observed that there are now a large number of advertisements aimed at encouraging women to drink – at persuading you that it is a glamorous and exciting thing to do. At the same time, the brewers have deliberately redecorated their pubs to make them more attractive to women.

Apart from these social and economic reasons, women may have individual problems in our society which make them turn to alcohol. The stresses of carrying out the dual roles of wage-earner and housewife/mother which many women experience today might be a factor here. New, 'emancipated' roles are not clearly defined and some women may feel guilty about abandoning their traditional responsibilities in the home. The 'empty nest' syndrome when all the children have left home, combined with the onset of the menopause, may create special problems for some middle-aged women and they may seek relief through drinking.

But, to finish on a more positive note, it should always be remembered that, in nearly every country in the world, women drink less than men and have fewer alcohol problems than men. So they deserve some credit! Yes, women do have some special concerns regarding alcohol and it is important that they are fully informed about these. But as long as you keep within the recommended, 'sensible' levels of drinking and heed the advice we offer in this chapter, there is certainly no need for alarm.

"I can lick any woman in the house!"

6
WHY DO I DRINK?

Alcohol has almost as many uses as it has users. It serves different purposes at different times. The drink you have on the way home from work will probably be for different reasons than the one you take on a Saturday night. On the next page you will find a list of questions about reasons for drinking. Look over this list very carefully and then tick 'Seldom' or 'Often' for each of the reasons. It is essential to answer as honestly as you can.

Why do I drink ?

	Seldom	Often
1. I drink because it helps me to relax.		
2. I drink because it is refreshing.		
3. I drink because it makes me feel good.		
4. I drink because of pressure from friends and workmates.		
5. I drink because it is polite to do so on certain occasions.		
6. I drink because I enjoy the taste.		
7. I drink because people I know drink.		
8. I drink in order to celebrate.		
9. I drink to forget my worries.		
10. I drink because it gives me confidence.		
11. I drink when I feel angry.		
12. I drink to be sociable.		
13. I drink because there is nothing else to do.		
14. I drink to pull myself together.		
15. I drink because it makes me feel at ease with people.		

If you have other reasons for drinking write them down below

16. I drink...

17. I drink...

18. I drink...

19. I drink...

20. I drink...

We will now go over each of the reasons for drinking in turn and discuss the good and bad aspects of each one. When you come to each discussion, look back to remind yourself what you have answered for that particular reason. You will find that, for several of the reasons, we suggest an alternative to alcohol which will be explained in more detail in Chapter 8. So please make a note of which of these alternatives is going to apply to you.

1. 'I drink because it helps me to relax.'

Most people who drink have enjoyed the pleasant, relaxing effects of alcohol in the company of friends. This is undoubtedly one of the main reasons why alcohol has been drunk for thousands of years all over the world. However, if you have ticked 'Often' for this reason, you must ask yourself how much you need alcohol in order to relax. You must ask yourself this question because it is too easy to come to use alcohol as you use tranquillizers – and alcohol is *at least* as dangerous as tranquillizers if you come to depend on it in the same way. There are other ways of relaxing which do not involve drugs and we will describe these in Chapter 8.

2. 'I drink because it is refreshing.'

This is a good reason for drinking because it is a positive reason. If you answered 'Often' here, you are not drinking because of a need and so you are not in danger of drinking too much when a need is not satisfied. However, as you may recall from Chapter 3, alcohol is mainly a depressant drug. So how can it be refreshing? The answer is that a small amount of alcohol (one or two units) seems like a stimulant in the short term; it makes you feel more alert and hence refreshed. But once you drink more than this, alcohol begins to have a depressant effect again.

3. 'I drink because it makes me feel good.'

What was said about reason 1 also applies here. If you begin to need alcohol in order to feel good, and especially if it becomes difficult to feel good without alcohol, you have a problem.

73

4. 'I drink because of pressure from friends and workmates.'

Drinking is a social custom and most of us enjoy drinking with friends. But sometimes pressure from other people can lead you to drink more than you would choose to drink on your own. This is perhaps one reason why sales representatives have high rates of drinking problems – in order to do business, they often have to drink with their customers. So, as with most of the reasons in this chapter, this reason for drinking is a two-edged sword. And if you have friends, relatives or workmates who are heavy drinkers, the chances are they will try to make you a heavy drinker too. Why? Because heavy drinkers often feel threatened by those who drink moderately since they are secretly worried about their own drinking. We will discuss how to cope with pressure to drink in Chapter 8.

5. 'I drink because it is polite to do so on certain occasions.'

You always have the choice not to drink alcohol if you do not wish to. 'I don't want a drink tonight' should be as acceptable as 'I don't smoke'. If your drinking companions give you a hard time over this, you should ask yourself why you bother meeting them for a drink.

6. 'I drink because I enjoy the taste.'

A good reason for drinking. But note that heavy drinking is out under this reason because high BACs dull the brain's capacity to distinguish different tastes.

© Hargreaves

7. 'I drink because people I know drink.'

What was said about reason 4 applies here too. Remember that you always have the choice about how much you drink, and you should ask yourself how often you drink more than you would choose to because your companions want to drink heavily. Round-buying makes this especially likely to happen, because rounds ensure that everyone in the company drinks at the rate of the heaviest drinker! And if he or she is 15 stones and highly tolerant to alcohol (see pages 38–39), what he or she can drink without getting drunk may cause serious problems for lighter-weight or less experienced drinkers.

8. 'I drink in order to celebrate.'

Another good reason for drinking, as long as you do not find cause for celebration several times a week.

9. 'I drink to forget my worries.'

If you have answered 'Often' for this reason, you have a potential problem with your drinking. Many people occasionally get drunk in order to get rid of tension and have a 'blow out'. But if you begin to use alcohol regularly for this purpose, you will probably make your worries and problems worse. Alcohol is likely to make you feel *more* depressed and anxious in the long-term. Also, if you drink rather than face up to your worries, you are less likely to be able to do something about them. Finally, drinking for this reason increases the risk that you will become dependent on alcohol. There are other ways of dealing with worry and anxiety than by drinking, and we will describe them in Chapter 8.

10. 'I drink because it gives me confidence.'

As with reason 9, this reason for drinking has more negative sides to it than positive. Fair enough, you may very occasionally drink for confidence on special occasions, such as making a speech at a wedding, but if you begin to *need* alcohol in more everyday affairs, then beware! If you feel shy, awkward or uncomfortable in company, you may find some of the advice in Chapter 8 helpful.

11. 'I drink when I feel angry.'

If you have answered 'Often' to this reason, you must ask yourself why you are drinking rather than trying to change whatever it is that is making you feel angry. Perhaps you will say that you cannot change what makes you angry. But if that is the case, then drinking may well become a problem for you because you will need it a lot of the time to feel better. It often happens that those who have difficulty in asserting themselves – that is, saying things which may be unpleasant to the listener – become heavy drinkers. This is because alcohol can be a substitute for standing up for yourself. See Chapter 8 for a discussion of ways of dealing with this problem.

12. 'I drink to be sociable.'

See the discussion of reasons 4, 5 and 7.

13. 'I drink because there is nothing else to do.'

If you ticked 'Often' for this reason, take care. If drinking is the main way of occupying yourself, when you suddenly have a lot of spare time on your hands for some reason, your drinking may well increase. This will probably cause problems and you may find it difficult to cut down again. See Chapter 8 for a discussion of other ways of dealing with boredom.

'Just what I say – nothing else to do, is there?'

© Alex Graham

LDYH–F

76

14. 'I drink to pull myself together.'

Another dangerous reason. Firstly, because it does not work in the long-term (in fact, it has the opposite effect) and secondly, because drinking to satisfy a need such as this may lead to a gradual increase in your drinking and possibly dependence on alcohol. Why is it you need pulling together? Can you not cope with stress in some other way than by drinking (see Chapter 8)?

15. 'I drink because it makes me feel at ease with other people.'

This is true for many drinkers, because alcohol is like an oil which makes the conversation flow a little more smoothly. But, once more, if you begin to find it hard to enjoy company without alcohol, then this is a dangerous reason. This is especially true if you need alcohol in order to talk to someone of the opposite sex. See Chapter 8 for a discussion of such difficulties.

Other reasons for drinking

You may have thought of other reasons for drinking which we have not mentioned and you may have written some down on the list of reasons given. There are literally hundreds of possibilities.

For example, some people use alcohol to help them get off to sleep. This is a tricky one because of tolerance. If you take a certain amount of alcohol regularly to make you sleep, it will gradually lose its effect. You will need more to achieve the same effect. Thus your drinking can grow out of proportion. The same is true if you use alcohol to relieve pain.

In general terms, using alcohol to relieve unpleasant feelings or to overcome personal difficulties is very risky. We discuss other ways of coping with these problems in Chapter 8.

Drinking as a habit

Although much drinking has reasons behind it, drinking is also very much a habit. The more you drink, the more it becomes habitual and the less it has to do with the original reasons for drinking.

Someone who has become physically dependent on alcohol drinks almost totally habitually and, as we all know, habits are very difficult to break. This is why some people with no apparent personal difficulties can become dependent on alcohol.

Almost everyone who takes alcohol is to some extent drinking habitually but the more you drink, the more true this is. In the next chapter, we explain how you can set about **breaking the habit.**

7
HOW CAN I CUT DOWN?

Before you can cut down your drinking, obviously you must have made the decision that you want to. In Chapter 2 you wrote a list of reasons why you needed to cut down and you also made a contract with yourself to try your hardest to do so. Now look back at Chapter 2 to remind yourself that the reasons you put down were good ones.

*   *   *   *   *

We have found that it is easier for people to stick to decisions they have made if they tell others about these decisions. So why not tell your husband or wife, friends or other people who are important to you that you are going to try to cut down your drinking? Tick the appropriate places in the box below.

Tell other people

Which of these people are you going to tell about your decision to cut down your drinking?

Your Husband or Wife?	Your Boyfriend or Girlfriend ?
Yes No	Yes No
Your Friends or Workmates ?	Your Relatives or Close Friends ?
Yes No	Yes No

Your self-monitoring diary

Before you can break a habit, you must be **aware** of it. This is because habits are often unconscious – you are not aware of them. But to change them, you must become conscious of them.

So the first step in cutting down your drinking is to start what is called **self-monitoring.** All this means is watching yourself and keeping a diary of when, where and exactly how much you drink. You have already done this to some extent for the last typical week of drinking in Chapter 2. But what you should do from today is to note down every time you have a drink on the Drinking Diary sheets in Appendix B at the back of the book.

As an example, a day in the Drinking Diary might look like the entry below.

Drinking Diary

WEEK 1

Day	Time	Hours Spent	Place	Who with	Other Activiites	Money Spent	Consequences (if any)	Units
Thursday	1-2	1	Nag's Head	Tom	Eating	1.60	Sleepy	10
	5-6	1	The Bull	Jim Tom	—	2.40	—	
	8-12	4	Social Club	Jim Bob	Darts	9.00	hangover	
day	1-2	1	The Bull	Tom	Eating	1.40	—	

The columns of the Diary are easy to understand but perhaps the column 'Consequences' requires some comment. Although the examples given might be regarded as bad consequences of drinking, this need not always be the case. You can enter good consequences as well. For instance, 'met inter-

80

esting new people' might be a good consequence of drinking.

It is also clear from the example that you should make a separate entry for each drinking session in a day. So, if you have a drink at lunchtime and go out again in the evening, you should not lump these two sessions together, but should record each one separately in the Diary.

Over the next 12 weeks, keep a record of your drinking every day.
Do not wait until the end of the week to fill in the Diary sheets. *Fill them in as soon after drinking as possible,* because otherwise you might forget to record all your drinks.

It is also a good idea to make a note of how much you have while you are actually drinking. Just put a tick in a notebook or on a piece of paper for every unit of alcohol you drink. That way you can be absolutely sure you don't forget anything. Even better is to make a note before you decide to order a drink or tell somebody what you want, because this ensures that you make a deliberate decision to have another drink rather than just drifting into it without thinking. At the very least, you should try to jot down what you drink before you start drinking it.

Later on, in the privacy of your home, you can transfer what you have recorded onto the Diary sheets in this book.

Even after you have completed all the Diary pages in the book, you should still record in a pocket diary how many units of alcohol you drink each day. Only by keeping a close track of your drinking will you be able to see if your intake is beginning to creep up again.

So, start today to record all the alcoholic drinks you have in the Drinking Diary in Appendix B.

Risky circumstances

Do you sometimes find that you drink more than you intended to?

Do you sometimes end up regretting how much you drank the day before?

81

Does your drinking sometimes get you into trouble?

If so, we will now try to find out whether there are any particular circumstances associated with the times when you drank more than you think you should have. In other words, we will be looking for *risky circumstances* which are connected with your drinking.

The way to do this is to look at the last few times when drinking caused you trouble – hangovers, accidents, lateness for work, arguments in the family, etc. – as well as the last few times when you drank without trouble. Is there anything which distinguishes the two types of drinking episode? Look at the examples on the next page of how one man completed two tables asking about troublesome and troublefree drinking episodes. (Note that the tables are made up in the same way as your Drinking Diary.)

Troublesome Drinking Times

	Day Date	Time	Hours Spent	Place	Who with	Other Activities	Units	Money Spent	Consequences (If any)
TIME 1	Fri	6-11 pm	5	Archie's flat The Bull	Archie, Bill, Colin	none	12	£ 7.00	Fell, cut my hand
TIME 2	Sat	5-10 pm	5	Kate's Bar Chinese Rest.	Bill, Colin	Fruit machine	10	£ 6.00	Argument with Bill – Home early
TIME 3	Thur	7-11 pm	4	Social Club	Darts team	none	10	£ 5.50	Hangover – late for work next day
TIME 4	Sat	6-12 pm	6	Social Club	Colin, Alastair	none	12	£ 7.00	Missed bus home argument with wife

Trouble Free Drinking Times

	Day Date	Time	Hours Spent	Place	Who with	Other Activities	Units	Money Spent	Consequences (If any)
TIME 1	Thur	8-11 pm	3	Social Club	Darts team	Darts	6	£ 3.00	
TIME 2	Fri	8-12 pm	4	Chinese Rest. Eagle Bar	Wife, Betty, Bill	Eating	5	£ 2.50	
TIME 3	Sat	9-12 pm	3	Social Club	Bill, Archie	Dominoes	4	£ 2.00	
TIME 4	Sun	8-11 pm	3	Kate's Bar	Alastair, John	None	6	£ 3.50	

Write down the circumstances common to the times when the man's drinking caused problems. Do this before reading the man's answers on the next page.

1. _____

2. _____

3. _____

4. _____

5. _____

Now write down the circumstances common to his trouble free drinking.

1. _____

2. _____

3. _____

4. _____

5. _____

TROUBLESOME TIMES

1. He always began drinking at 7pm or earlier when he got into trouble.

2. Colin was with him on each of these occasions.

3. Three out of the four times, he drank for more than four hours.

4. Each time, he drank 10 units or more.

5. Three out of four times he wasn't doing anything besides drinking.

TROUBLE FREE TIMES

1. He always began drinking at 8pm or later.

2. Colin was never with him on these occasions.

3. He always drank for four hours or less.

4. He never drank more than 6 units of alcohol.

5. Three out of four times, he was doing something else as well as drinking.

In this example, troublesome drinking was associated with certain risky circumstances. The individual in question made certain rules for himself on the basis of the information in the tables:

My Drinking Rules

1. I will never drink alcohol before 8pm at night.
2. I will stop drinking with Colin.
3. I will never drink over a period of more than four hours.
4. I will never drink more than 6 units in one day.
5. I will try to combine drinking with some other pleasant activity such as eating, darts or dominoes.

Find your own 'risky times': risky circumstances can be of several different kinds:

People you drink with – including those with whom you tend to drink too much and those with whom you tend to control your drinking.

Times when you drink – including times of the day and certain days of the week, like weekends.

Whether you are thirsty or hungry.

How you feel emotionally – whether you are anxious or under stress, frustrated and angry or depressed.

Conflicts with other people – this may include rows with wife or husband, or brushes with the boss and so on.

There are many other kinds of risky circumstances, including those which apply to you alone and to nobody else. You may be able to think of some personal circumstances connected with your drinking which are risky for you.

Now try to do this exercise for your own drinking. First, think back to the last four times when your drinking either caused you trouble or when you felt you drank too much. Fill in the first chart. Then think about the last four times when you drank without trouble or regret and fill in the details on the second chart.

Then see whether there is anything common to the first four occasions and anything common to the second four, and write these common features down. Write as many or as few as you can find. (Don't worry if you can only find one or two.)

86

Troublesome Drinking Times

	Day Date	Time	Hours Spent	Place	Who with	Other Activities	Units	Money Spent	Consequences (if any)
TIME 1									
TIME 2									
TIME 3									
TIME 4									

Trouble Free Drinking Times

	Day Date	Time	Hours Spent	Place	Who with	Other Activities	Units	Money Spent	Consequences (if any)
TIME 1									
TIME 2									
TIME 3									
TIME 4									

What do my troublesome drinking sessions have in common?

1.

2.

3.

4.

5.

What do my trouble free drinking sessions have in common?

1.

2.

3.

4.

5.

Now fill in 'My Drinking Rules' on the next page.

My Drinking Rules

1. _____

2. _____

3. _____

4. _____

5. _____

The Drinking Rules you have just written down will be based on drinking episodes in the past. However, you can also use the Drinking Diary sheets in Appendix B to do the exercise all over again in about six weeks' time, and change your Drinking Rules if necessary. We provide instructions on how to do this in a separate appendix at the end of the book (Appendix C).

A word of explanation

You have now made some rules about your drinking. But why is it that you feel the urge to drink more in some circumstances than in others?

One answer to this question is *conditioning*. This means that you learn to associate particular situations with the urge to drink. For instance, if in the past you have often gone for a drink on the way home from work, in the future you will feel a special urge to drink when you have finished work. If in the past you have often got drunk with certain friends, when you meet them in the future, you are more likely to feel the urge to get drunk with them again.

Hence, what you must learn to do now is to avoid those situations where in the past you have drunk heavily or got into some kind of trouble. At the same time, you must also confine your drinking to those situations where in the past you have drunk moderately and without problems. The Drinking Rules which you wrote on page 89 are aimed at helping you to do precisely this.

One more rule

In your Drinking Rules you may or may not have written down a rule about what the maximum amount you are allowed to drink on any one occasion should be. In the example on page 83, the man had no trouble when he drank less than about 6 units of alcohol. Therefore, one of his rules was that he should never drink more than this amount (although he should mostly try to keep well below this level). Have you made a similar 'cut-off point' for your own drinking?

If you haven't got a cut-off point for your drinking, then you should have one. We will explain here how to decide what this maximum limit in any one day should be.

The first thing to note is that the cut-off must obviously represent a reduction in your drinking. More than that, it must be a meaningful reduction – not just one or two units, but a sizeable drop in intake.

On the other hand, you must set yourself a realistic figure. There is no point in setting your cut-off so low that there is never any chance that you are going to stick to it. Also, although we have been examining drinking episodes when thinking about risky circumstances, it is much easier to set your cut-off for the whole day. Therefore, the cut-off has got to be able to include the possibility of more than one drinking episode in a day. For both these reasons, try to set a *realistic* cut-off.

To help you narrow down to actual figures, we strongly recommend that the cut-off you choose *must never be above 8 units per day*. And even then this should be spaced over a long period of time – over five hours. You will normally be spending less time on drinking than this. Therefore the conclusion is that your cut-off should be lower than 8 units in any one day.

To come right down to it, we had better give you straightforward advice about where you should fix your cut-off point.

This will depend on your sex, for reasons which have already been covered (see Chapter 5).

For men, we recommend that your cut-off point is between 4 and 8 units.

For women, we recommend that your cut-off point is between 3 and 5 units.

Note that a cut-off does not mean that you should drink that amount every day. Not at all! On most days you should drink much less than your cut-off, and we hope that on several days a week you will not drink at all. The cut-off is simply the amount you should never exceed in one day.

A final point about your cut-off is that it must be combined with another maximum limit – the limit of 21 units for men and 14 units for women for your Grand Total for the week (see Chapter 2). Therefore, you must choose a daily cut-off which permits you to keep within the weekly limit for healthy drinking.

Let us now remind you of all the points to bear in mind when choosing a Daily Cut-off for yourself:

1. The cut-off point should represent a meaningful reduction in your drinking.

2. It should be a realistic target to aim for.

3. The cut-off should be a limit which may include more than one drinking episode in a day.

4. It should never be set above 8 units a day.

5. For men, we recommend a cut-off between 4 and 8 units in any one day.

6. For women, we recommend a cut-off between 3 and 5 units in any one day.

7. Your daily cut-off must be combined with a weekly limit of 21 units for men and 14 units for women.

8. If you have already made a cut-off in your Drinking Rules on page 89, look at it again and see if it needs to be changed in the light of this discussion.

My Daily Cut-Off is ....

Now, taking all these factors into account, decide on your **Daily Cut-off** and write it down.

.... UNITS

Slowing down your drinking

Even though you have set your daily cut-off and even though you may be beginning to drink in less risky circumstances, you may still be having difficulties. One common difficulty is in slowing down your drinking. If you want to drink less but still want to enjoy other people's company while drinking, *you must drink more slowly.*

This can be difficult because drinking is a habit and, as we have said several times before, habits are very hard to break. Here are some hints about how to change your drinking habits by slowing down your intake.

1. Pace yourself.
How much do you plan to drink?
How long do you intend to be drinking for?
How long must each drink last?

Answer these questions each time before you drink. For example, your answers might be:

I plan to drink 6 units (3 pints) tonight. I will go out at 8.30 p.m. and come back at 11 p.m. Therefore, three pints must last 2 1/2 hours divided by three, which roughly equals one pint every 50 minutes.

Fifty minutes for a pint? You may think this is impossible, but you can learn to do it with the help of some of the following hints.

2. Take smaller sips.

As well as planning how long each drink should take, slow down the rate at which you sip your drink. Sip less often and take smaller sips. Count the number of sips it takes to finish your glass. Then try increasing the number on the next glass. Then try to better that, and so on. You can imagine that you are trying to break your 'personal best' record each time.

3. Put your glass down between sips.

Don't warm your drink in your hand. Put it down on a table or shelf after each sip. If it's in your hand, you'll probably drink more often.

4. Occupy yourself.

Don't just drink! Do something else enjoyable while you are drinking that will help distract you from the glass and drink more slowly. Here are a few things you can do: reading; chatting; playing games such as darts, pool, draughts, dominoes, etc.; eating (but beware of crisps and peanuts because they make you more thirsty); listening to music.

5. Change your drink.

Remember conditioning? Old familiar drinks of your heavy drinking days will give you the urge to drink like that again. So be adventurous. Try stout instead of bitter. Try lager instead of stout. What about wine? If you drink spirits, change to a different type and make it a long drink by adding orange, tonic or other mixers. The only thing to beware of is choosing new drinks which are stronger than you imagine. Find out the strength of everything you try. But remember: *give up the old 'heavy-drinking' drinks*.

6. Drink for the taste.

Savour the taste of your drink. Let it rest on the tongue and enjoy the flavour. Don't just swill it down!

7. Don't drink beer and spirits together.

Why not? Because you take in alcohol much faster that way.

8. If you drink spirits, dilute them.
The longer the drink, the slower the rate of alcohol ingestion. So top up drinks with non-alcoholic mixers, preferably by adding more mixer than you have spirits.

9. What about rounds?
If you regularly drink in a round-buying group, ask yourself whether you are drinking more than you would choose to if you were not in a round. There are a number of hints for dealing with this tricky problem.

Why not say to the group that you will buy your own drinks and explain why? If they reject you because of this, were they worthwhile friends anyway? If this is difficult, buy one round (so that they know you aren't mean) and then go 'solo'. Or, you can simply not buy yourself a drink when it is your turn to buy. That way, of course, you save money and drink less. Or, just refuse drinks every so often and accept the fact that you will pay out more than you will drink. If you get too drunk, you won't appreciate the extra alcohol anyway.

Finally, ask yourself whether this group in which you drink might be a 'risky circumstance' which should be avoided. If this is the case, perhaps the easiest way of avoiding rounds is to drop out of the group and drink with other, smaller groups of people. You might be amazed to find that someone else in the group feels the way you do. Try talking to some of them on their own and see.

10. Try a 'spacer' instead of a 'chaser'.
A 'spacer' is a non-alcoholic drink which you take in between alcoholic ones – you space them out. That way you slow down your rate of drinking alcohol. If you have never tried this, you will be surprised how refreshing a spacer can be. Alternatively, you could try a low alcohol beer.

11. Imitate the slow drinker.
Is there somebody in the pub or in your company at home who drinks slowly? If so, watch them. Become their shadow. Don't pick up the glass till they do. Take the same small sips

they take. In between sips, do something else with your hands instead of lifting the glass to your lips. Try to make as good an imitation of the slow drinker as you can.

Rewarding your successes

If you think about it, most of this chapter so far has been concerned with making rules. You have written down your personal Drinking Rules on page 89 and you have also made a rule about the cut-off for your drinking on any one day on page 92. We hope you have also made a rule to yourself about keeping your Drinking Diary up-to-date every day. What is more, all the things we discussed in the last section which were aimed at helping you slow down your drinking can be thought of as setting yourself rules about the way you drink and trying to stick to them.

In this section, we will advise you how to make it easier to stick to the rules you have made. We are concerned here with rewarding yourself every time you successfully obey one of your rules. There are four ways in which you can reward your successes and we will take each in turn.

1. Material rewards

These can be almost anything you like, but there are a few things to bear in mind when choosing a material reward.

(a) It should be something that can be given fairly soon after your success. The sooner you get the reward, the more effective it is in supporting your new behaviour.

(b) It should be something you can easily get and afford.

(c) On the other hand, it should be something over and above the normal pleasures of life – something which is a luxury.

(d) It should also be something which is a pleasure for you – not just something which is supposed to be a reward.

The kinds of thing that can serve as rewards are: CDs, tapes, books, magazines, games, gadgets, clothes, bits of furniture, food you don't normally allow yourself; special treats like going to a good restaurant, the cinema, the theatre, a concert, etc.; other things you don't often do, like making a long-distance telephone call, visiting a special friend or trying a hobby you really enjoy. There are lots of things which can be used as rewards, depending on your own tastes. But you must be sensible in choosing rewards. If you are already overweight, more food is not a good idea. And, of course, you should never reward yourself for cutting down drinking by having another drink! Now write down five things or activities that could serve as material rewards for you in the spaces below.

1 _____   4 _____

2 _____   5 _____

3 _____

Another way of rewarding yourself is to build up small rewards gradually until they amount to something really special – something you have always wanted. A simple way of doing this is to work out each week how much you have saved on drink by cutting down. (You can use the 'Money Spent on Alcohol' column in your Drinking Diary for this.) Then put this amount away in a box, or in a special account at the bank, making a note of how much has been saved so far. When the total has reached a level you have decided on beforehand, you can spend it all on that special thing you really want. Using this method, you'll find it is very rewarding to watch your savings on drink mount up.

There are *two golden rules* to be observed in using material rewards. The first is that you must make an agreement with yourself beforehand as to what will count as a success and what reward you will give yourself for that success. To repeat, you must decide this beforehand and keep to it. It's no use deciding on a reward after you have succeeded. For example, you might make an agreement with yourself that, if you keep within your weekly Grand Total, you will reward yourself by going out for a curry to your favourite Indian restaurant. It will help you to keep to your agreement if you write it down somewhere.

The second golden rule is that you either succeed or fail: there are no in-betweens. For example, if you have set your daily cut-off at six units and you find that you have had eight on a particular day, you must not say to yourself, 'I nearly made it and I deserve that reward of a new record'. Stick rigidly to your limits and don't bend the rules. This applies to all the kinds of rewards we discuss here.

2. Mental rewards
This refers to talking to yourself in your head by 'singing your own praises' every time you successfully keep to a rule.

You may think this sounds crazy or childish but it is not. We know it to be a very effective way of changing your behaviour. The kinds of things you could say to yourself are as follow:

'I did really well to keep below my daily cut-off today.'

'I'm successfully keeping to my Drinking Rules and I'm getting more control over my drinking all the time.'

'I'm showing great perseverance in keeping my Drinking Diary up to date.'

'I succeeded very well in avoiding getting into that round and I must be getting healthier all the time.'

'I took more sips to drink that pint than I have ever managed before.'

These are just a few examples and, of course, you will be able to think of many more. But these examples do make the point that mental rewards can be used for the little successes you have during the day—like drinking a drink slowly, avoiding getting into a round, politely refusing a drink, and so on.

You can also use mental rewards for your larger achievements, such as keeping to your daily cut-off or your weekly limit. The great advantage of these mental rewards is that they don't cost a penny!

Now write down in the spaces given a few things that you could say to yourself as rewards for keeping to your rules. We suggest you concentrate on the obvious benefits of cutting down drinking, like looking and feeling healthier, feeling fitter, avoiding troubles from drinking, having more time to do useful things, and so on.

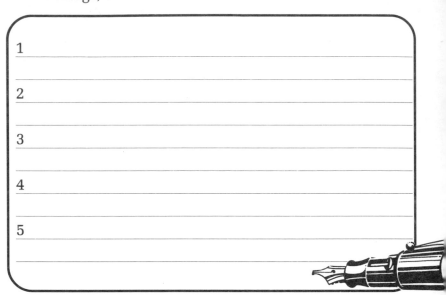

1

2

3

4

5

If you fail to keep to your limits or you break other rules you have made, this is no reason to become depressed or give up trying. Instead, try to think of the lessons you can learn from the experience and how you can change things in the future. Remind yourself of all the unpleasant consequences if you continue to drink too much, including those listed in Chapter 4, and of what may happen to you if you do not succeed in cutting down your drinking.

These warnings to yourself can also be used if you feel the temptation to go over a limit or break some other rule – remember all the frightening things that could happen to you if you go back to your old ways, and then give yourself a mental 'pat on the back' for having fought off the temptation.

3. A partner in reward

As well as mental and material rewards, you can also use another person to give you rewards for your drinking achievements. Choose someone close to you whom you trust and who knows all about your efforts to cut down your drinking. It should obviously not be someone who will take the opportunity to criticize or insult you.

There are several ways in which your partner can be of help to you in cutting down. First of all, you can make an agreement with them that they will only reward you in some way if you keep to a rule. Remember that the reward should be something special, like cooking you a favourite meal or treating you to a night out. Also, you might agree to enjoy a certain reward together.

Apart from rewarding separate successes, your partner can also be of great help by going over your progress with you – for example, by discussing the difficulties you have come across and congratulating your successes. It could be very helpful if your trusted partner reads this book with you in order to understand exactly what you are trying to do.

There are two ways in which you should definitely not use a partner. Firstly, you should not ask him or her to act as a kind of policeman by checking up on whether you have kept a rule or not. That must be entirely your own responsibility. Secondly, you should never use your partner for any kind of punishment for not keeping to a rule, because this can harm a good relationship.

4. Charting your progress

There is nothing so rewarding as being able to see clearly the progress you have made. For this reason we have supplied a graph for you to use in Appendix D at the end of the book to record the amount you drink week by week.

Naturally, it is the more mathematically inclined who will think first of filling in this graph but, actually, anybody can use it. If you follow the instructions in Appendix D, it is very simple indeed. We recommend you to chart your progress on the graph because we know that this too is an effective way of helping you to cut down. You will be able to sit back and gloat at your successes and you will also be able to notice when you are sliding back into your bad old ways again. So do give it a try.

More hints for cutting down

Here are some more things you can do to help you cut down your drinking.

Eating

Try always to eat properly before drinking. You don't 'waste' the alcohol if you do; rather, it is absorbed more slowly and gives you a more pleasant sensation than if you drink on an empty stomach. If you eat crisps and peanuts while you are drinking, always have a non-alcoholic 'spacer' with them – otherwise they will make you thirsty and you will drink more alcohol. Spacers in between alcoholic drinks also act like a 'food' which slows down the absorption of alcohol.

Start later

If you have not already made a Drinking Rule for yourself about when to drink, think about starting drinking later than usual. Instead of going to the pub at eight, go at nine o'clock. If you usually have a drink before your evening meal, miss it out – at least sometimes.

Learn to refuse drinks

Remember, you are the one who decides when, where and how much you drink. So rehearse ways of refusing drinks. For example, 'No thanks, I'm cutting down'; or, 'Not tonight, I've got a bad stomach'; or, 'Sorry, doctor's orders.' If people persist, ask yourself why they are so keen to see you drinking more than you want to.

If you find refusing drinks difficult, you can practise by play-acting with a trusted friend or relation whom you have taken into your confidence.

Know how much you have drunk

This is just a reminder about self-monitoring. Try to make a note of every drink you have before you drink it and enter it later on in your Drinking Diary. If you are at a party, measure out your drinks carefully. (You can practise measuring out a unit of alcohol, so that you become familiar with how much there is in each drink, by following the instructions on page 15.) Another thing – don't fill your glass until it's empty, otherwise you may lose track of what you have drunk. And fill in your Drinking Diary every day.

But I need to drink!

Is this true for you? If so, why? Is it because you are tense, anxious, depressed, shy, bored, lonely, lacking in confidence ...? If so, then drink is not the answer.

In the next chapter, we discuss some of these problems and how you can solve them without the aid of alcohol.

Days of rest

If you drink every day, then your body and mind will miss it when you don't have a drink for whatever reason. If you never take a day off from alcohol, you may well lack confidence about being able to break the habit. Abstaining on at least a couple of days a week both boosts your confidence and helps you enjoy your tipple more when you do take it.

Another reason for staying dry some days in the week is that you can learn to enjoy doing things without alcohol. Many people believe that they cannot talk easily to strangers or mix at a social gathering unless they have a drink. Because they do believe this, they always take a drink when meeting other people. What they never discover, because they never try it out, is that they can mix without alcohol. Similarly, some people never give themselves a chance to develop other interests, skills, sports or hobbies because their time is all taken up with drinking.

So experiment! What about that car maintenance class you were always talking about? You have always wanted to play a musical instrument, so go out and buy a guitar and a teach yourself book. Why not start with a little exercise or take up a sport? Nothing makes you want to cut down so much as trying to get fit.

There are hundreds of opportunities which you may be

'Well, before we do business, let's have a little drink.'

missing. Give yourself a chance! For all these reasons, as well as for reasons of health, abstain from alcohol for at least two days a week and preferably more.

A summary

Now let us summarize what you have learned by going over all the methods you can use for cutting down. There are some things, like keeping your Drinking Diary, sticking to your Drinking Rules and setting yourself a strict Daily Cut-off, which are absolutely essential.

The other methods are optional and whether you use some or all of them depends on the details of your individual situation. But you must be patient and give each method a good try. Also, it will help if you try one at a time and gradually add each method to your way of drinking.

On page 104 is a list of all the methods for cutting down we have discussed in this chapter. Put a tick opposite each one according to whether you will definitely use it, whether you might use it, or whether you will not use it. (To remind yourself, read over your Drinking Rules on page 89.) This exercise is not binding and you can always change your mind later and use a method you have not tried before. The point of checking the list now is to encourage you to think clearly and make deliberate decisions about the methods you will employ in the attempt to cut down.

Methods for Cutting Down

Keep a Drinking Diary	Yes	Maybe	No
Keep to my personal Drinking Rules	Yes	Maybe	No
Keep under a Daily Cut-off of alcohol	Yes	Maybe	No
Keep under my weekly Grand Total of 21 units (men), 14 units (women)	Yes	Maybe	No

You should have definitely ticked 'Yes' for the first four items

Pace my drinking	Yes	Maybe	No
Sip more slowly	Yes	Maybe	No
Take smaller sips	Yes	Maybe	No
Occupy myself while drinking	Yes	Maybe	No
Change my type of drink	Yes	Maybe	No
Drink for the taste	Yes	Maybe	No
Don't mix beer and spirits	Yes	Maybe	No
Imitate the slow drinker	Yes	Maybe	No
Put my glass down between sips	Yes	Maybe	No
Tell my friends I'll buy my own drinks	Yes	Maybe	No
Buy one round and then go 'solo'	Yes	Maybe	No
Give myself material rewards for successes	Yes	Maybe	No
Give myself mental rewards for successes	Yes	Maybe	No
Ask someone close to be my partner in reward	Yes	Maybe	No
Chart my progress on the graphs provided	Yes	Maybe	No
Order a spacer	Yes	Maybe	No
Refuse drinks during some rounds	Yes	Maybe	No
Give up drinking with round-buying groups	Yes	Maybe	No
Dilute my spirits	Yes	Maybe	No
Eat before I drink	Yes	Maybe	No
Buy soft drinks in between alcoholic ones	Yes	Maybe	No
Take at least two days rest from alcohol per week	Yes	Maybe	No
Start drinking later	Yes	Maybe	No
Learn to refuse drinks	Yes	Maybe	No

TICK THIS CHART, THEN READ IT EVERY DAY TO REMIND
YOURSELF OF THE DECISIONS YOU HAVE MADE

8
ALTERNATIVES TO ALCOHOL

**It would be wrong to pretend that there are easy
answers to all of life's problems, but in this chapter we
will try to help you look at some of the difficulties you
may be facing and suggest ways to make the most of
your life without excessive drinking.**

*   *   *   *   *

As we saw in Chapter 6, drinking because you need to drink
is a bad idea because it can lead to dependence on alcohol.
Look back to your answers to 'Why do I drink?' on page 72
and consider to what extent you are drinking for reasons of
need. There are many different needs or problems which can
lead to heavy drinking, but perhaps the four most common
can be remembered by the first four letters of the alphabet;
Anxiety, Boredom, Confidence, Depression.

In this chapter we discuss ways of setting about coping
with these common problems, together with other difficulties
such as marital disharmony, sexual problems and insomnia.
You may not want to read about all these problems if you
think they have no relevance to your situation, but it would
do no harm to quickly look over the whole chapter. You can
then come back and study those sections which most apply to
yourself.

Anxiety

Alcohol is a depressant drug and hence it depresses the activity of the nervous system, making you feel less anxious. But
this is only true in the short term. When they drink a lot, most
people begin to get hangovers, which in turn make them feel
anxious and depressed. Therefore, in the long term, heavy
drinking can make you more anxious and you get caught in a
vicious circle of drinking to relieve anxiety, which in turn

makes you more anxious, leading to further drinking and so on. Use the box to compare some common symptoms of anxiety and common hangover symptoms.

ANXIETY	HANGOVER
SHAKINESS	SHAKING HANDS
DIARRHOEA	DIARRHOEA
POOR CONCENTRATION	POOR CONCENTRATION
LOSS OF APPETITE	LOSS OF APPETITE
SWEATING	SWEATING
TENSION	
HEADACHE	HEADACHE
PALPITATIONS	TREMORS
DIZZINESS	
STOMACH UPSET	STOMACH UPSET
BREATHLESSNESS	

Do you see the similarities? If you drink heavily (more than 21 units a week for men and 14 units a week for women), then you are more likely to experience anxiety-like symptoms which are caused by alcohol – even though you may think you are drinking to get rid of anxiety. Remember, drinking to get rid of anxiety can lead to alcohol dependence.

So how can you get rid of anxiety without turning to alcohol? This book cannot give complete answers but it can point you in various directions which may be of help.

Fear of fear

Before we describe some methods of reducing anxiety, it must be pointed out that anxiety can sometimes be stoked up by fear of the symptoms of the anxiety itself. In other words, people can worry too much about the symptoms of anxiety

106

described in the box – by sleep problems, a pounding heart, dizziness, etc. *But these symptoms are not dangerous.* If you just try to detach yourself from them a little, they will disappear. On the other hand, if you worry about them, they will persist. Sometimes people fear that these symptoms are signs that they are 'cracking up' or 'going mad'. *Anxiety has nothing whatever to do with 'madness'.* People whom you may think of as 'mad' have completely different problems which have nothing to do with anxiety.

Breathing
You tend to breathe quickly when you feel anxious and this, again, can make you feel more anxious still. Shallow, quick breathing is called 'hyperventilation' and causes anxiety-type symptoms. Try deeper, slow breathing the next time you feel anxious. In fact, do it now:

1. Rest your fingers on the bottom of your rib cage and close your eyes.

2. Breathe in and out slowly and gently so that this part of your chest rises and falls.

3. Take one long, slow, inward breath, making sure your whole lungs are full.

4. Hold for three or four seconds.

5. Breathe out slowly and gently, and let your whole body relax as you exhale, saying 'Relax' to yourself as you do so .

6. Repeat this several times and as often as you want, without straining yourself.

7. Practise this a few times a day – it doesn't take long.

8. In between practice, try to breathe more slowly and a little more deeply.

Learning to relax
You may get tense when you are anxious. Muscle tension can cause headaches and make you tired. There are many ways of

learning to relax. For some people, simply lying back and listening to music is enough. But there are other ways which involve learning how to control the tension in your muscles. The principle is to know when your muscles are tense and when they are relaxed. You can learn to do this by the following steps:

1. **Tense up one group of muscles (say your neck muscles).**

2. **Notice what the feelings of tension are like.**

3. **Now relax the muscles.**

4. **Notice the different feelings when the muscles are relaxed.**

5. **Let these feelings and the relaxation increase.**

Do this for each group of muscles. For example, you might work through them like this:

right arm — left arm — neck — scalp — face — shoulders— back — chest —stomach — right leg — left leg

This needs lots of practice every day. Try practising in a quiet darkened room and leave yourself plenty of time. Fifteen minutes once or twice a day should be of help.

This brief outline of how to relax may not be enough for you. You can get further information and advice from these books:

Stress and Relaxation: Self-help Techniques for Everyone **by Jane Madders. Published by Optima (Positive Health Guide Series).**

The Relaxation Response **by H. Benson and M. Klipper. Published by Collins.**

Relaxation through exercise

Physical exercise – swimming, running, walking, football, badminton and a hundred other sports – is a great way of relaxing. If you take regular exercise, you will probably feel less tense and anxious. Why not try to start some form of exercise?. You can't think of any? Well, think back to your younger days. What sports or exercises have you done in the past? Write them down.

Sports or exercises I have done in the past

1 _____

2 _____

3 _____

4 _____

5 _____

Phobias

While on the subject of anxiety, there is one particular form of anxiety, known as a phobia, which can cause heavy drinking as well as other kinds of severe discomfort in the sufferer.

A phobia is an irrational fear of some object, situation or person. The sufferer knows it's irrational, but panics and tries to avoid the feared object whenever he or she encounters it. Common phobias are agoraphobia (fear of crowded places, of going out, of streets, etc.), dog phobia, snake phobia, wind phobia, acrophobia (fear of heights), thunder phobia and many others. Sometimes phobias can lead to heavy drinking because of the stress and anxiety they cause.

Phobias are usually amenable to treatment and the method most commonly used is to gradually and gently expose the person to the feared situation. So, for instance, a spider phobic would first be shown photographs of spiders until they no longer caused fear. Then toy spiders would be introduced until the person was used to them. Then dead spiders would be used until, finally, even live spiders would cause the person little discomfort.

If you have a phobia which is causing you problems, see your doctor about it and he or she will refer you to a psychologist or some other specialist who will be able to help you.

Loneliness and isolation
As we all know, loneliness can cause unhappiness and anxiety. If you are lonely or feel isolated, try to think how you can meet people without necessarily drinking heavily.

Are there any old friends you have drifted away from? That sometimes happens to heavy drinkers – they lose touch with old friends because drinking becomes more important than other things. How about looking your friends up again?

If you are unemployed or have too much time on your hands, you might like to go to your local Volunteer Bureau or Community Centre and ask whether you can do some voluntary work.

Do you need further help with anxiety?
If your anxiety is persistent and troublesome, your doctor may be able to refer you to someone who can help you. One of the following publications might also be helpful. (A bookshop will be able to order them for you.)

Self-Help for your Nerves by Clair Weeks. Published by Angus and Robertson.

Don't Panic: A Guide to Overcoming Panic Attacks by Sue Breton. Published by McDonald Optima.

Living with Fear: Understanding and Coping with Anxiety by Dr. Isaac M. Marks. Published by McGraw-Hill.

Boredom
Another problem which can be connected with heavy drinking is boredom. Have you ever said to yourself 'But there's nothing else to do around here except drink'? If you have, then think again, because it is not true. There is always something to do except drink, even though it might need some effort to arrange it.

Try some brainstorming. All this means is that you let your mind run free to come up with any ideas – no matter how ridiculous – about possible alternative activities to drinking. These can be anything from dominoes to tap-dancing, photography to flying. The important thing is not to check your ideas.

Try this exercise out with one of your family or a friend. Fill in the chart on page 112 with as many possible alternatives to drinking as you can come up with. Don't worry just now about whether or not you have the money or the opportunity to do them – just brainstorm!

Confidence

Some people drink because they lack confidence, feel shy or find it hard to stick up for themselves. People who find it difficult to be assertive are more likely to drink when they feel frustrated through not being able to stand up for themselves.

Often such people find it hard to express anger; they tend to bottle things up and say nothing, or say something different from what they feel. Sometimes they 'explode' much later in response to some trivial incident, when they should have been firmer at the time. They may have difficulty in saying 'no' to other people about things in general, including the offer of a drink. And sometimes these difficulties include shyness and low self-confidence, particularly in relation to the opposite sex.

We cannot deal with these problems properly here, though a few generalizations may help. First, 'confidence' or 'assertiveness' are skills, like driving a car or operating a machine. This means that with training and practice you can learn to behave in a more confident manner. And behaving more confidently makes you feel more confident. You can sometimes teach yourself these skills in the same way that you can teach yourself to operate a machine, but it is difficult. Two useful books in this area are:

When I Say No, I Feel Guilty by M.J. Smith. Published by Bantam Books.

How to Stand Up for Yourself by Dr. Paul Hauck. Published by Sheldon Press.

But if you feel that you lack confidence, why not try behaving as if you were confident a few times? If someone at work

Alternatives to Alcohol

1 _____	9 _____
2 _____	10 _____
3 _____	11 _____
4 _____	12 _____
5 _____	13 _____
6 _____	14 _____
7 _____	15 _____
8 _____	16 _____

Think carefully about the above alternatives. Which would you enjoy most? Can you do them locally? List below those activities you intend to take up.

1 _____	5 _____
2 _____	6 _____
3 _____	7 _____
4 _____	8 _____

Now make some notes on the first steps you will take to find out about these activities. (Contact local library, city information centre etc.)

alternative 1 _____   alternative 4 _____

alternative 2 _____   alternative 5 _____

alternative 3 _____   alternative 6 _____

asks you to do something which is not your job, stop and think. Do you normally say to yourself things like, 'I don't want to hurt his feelings by refusing'; or, 'It's too much trouble to refuse, I'll just do it'? If so, then what you are really saying is, 'I don't want to say no'; or, 'I'm scared to say no'.

Well, *try it and* see. Try asserting yourself a few times and you will be surprised that, in most cases, you'll feel much better for it and the results will be better than you feared. But take care not to go over the top! Assert yourself but don't lose your cool.

In some areas of the country you can also get help in social skills training groups, or assertion training groups. These are provided mostly by psychologists in the National Health Service and your doctor may be able to refer you to one. Some Councils on Alcohol (see Appendix A) offer them also.

© Mel Calman

I could be very dominating – if only someone would volunteer to be submissive . . .

Depression

Many people drink when they feel down. When you feel depressed for long periods, you can get 'stuck' in a very low emotional state. As we know, alcohol is a depressant and is guaranteed to make the problem worse in the long run. If you seem to have lost interest in things, if you don't seem to get any pleasure out of the things you used to enjoy, then perhaps you should see your doctor about it.

Depression responds well to both drug treatments and psychological treatments, if only you can drag yourself along for help. However, many people feel low at times without being depressed in a clinical sense – in the sense a doctor would use the term.

But it is still dangerous to use alcohol as a drug to combat depression. If you feel down, talk to someone about it. It's amazing how talking can help. If you can't confide in your friends or family, go to a clergyman, a doctor, a social worker or even a Citizen's Advice Bureau, because it may have details of counselling services in your area. Some Councils on Alcohol (see Appendix A) will offer you help though you may not be an alcoholic. Some GPs have counselling services too, so if in doubt talk to your doctor.

The important thing when you are feeling down is to find someone to talk to and don't drink alcohol. These books might also be of some use:

Depression by Jack Dominion. Published by Fontana.

The Element Guide to Depression by Sue Bretton. Published by Element.

Bereavement

Bereavement leads to depressive feelings for quite some time after the death of a loved one, sometimes for more than a year. This is a particularly dangerous time to start drinking heavily because you can get hooked on alcohol and when you stop grieving, you can't stop drinking heavily.

If you have been bereaved recently, try to find friends and counsellors to help you through this difficult time, and try to avoid using alcohol as a pain-reliever.

There is a self-help organization called CRUSE Bereavement Care which may be of help. Address: CRUSE House, 126 Sheen Road, Richmond, Surrey, TW9 1UR; Telephone Counselling Service (9.30am–5.00pm) 0181 332 7227.

Marriage problems

Marriage problems often lead to heavy drinking in both men and women. Sometimes these problems are used as an excuse for continued heavy drinking. Sometimes cause and effect get lost in a horrible jumble of nagging, quarrelling and bad feeling. Sometimes the drinking is itself the cause of the problem.

If you have marriage problems, *the important thing is to talk about them.* It is seldom that two people who live together actually sit down and talk about the things which are dividing them. Shouting and accusations take the place of real communication.

If you find that you cannot talk coolly about your problems, find a neutral person with whom you can talk things out. In addition to the types of people mentioned on page 114, you can also go to your local Marriage Guidance Council, the address of which will be in your telephone directory. You will be surprised how a detached view of your disagreements can help you to sort things out.

Sadly, however, many marriages end in divorce. Even if strife and unpleasantness have preceded separation, actual separation or divorce can lead to feelings akin to grief in those involved. Drinking during such times can be increased considerably. There are no easy answers to how to cope with these feelings, though some of the advice in this chapter about how to cope with depression, anxiety and loneliness may be useful. If you have a friend or someone else with whom you can talk at this time, it may be of considerable help.

The following books might also be of use:

Divorce for Beginners: How to get Unhitched Without the Hitches **by Cathy Hopkins. Published by Harper Collins.**

How to Survive Divorce **by Roy van den Brink-Budgen. Published by Published by How To Books.**

Sexual difficulties

Men who are heavy drinkers have more sexual problems than men who are not. This is largely because of the effects of alcohol which, in Shakespeare's immortal words, 'Provokes the desire, but takes away the performance.'

Some men and women drink heavily because of sexual difficulties. And, of course, drinking tends to make these difficulties worse. So sexual problems are both a cause and a result of heavy drinking.

Most sexual problems can be remedied by relatively simple methods. One of the basic ways of overcoming them is to make sure that the sexual relationship is based on a warm and open emotional relationship. And the key word here is communication. Talk about your sexual worries and problems with your partner. Discuss what you like and don't like about your sexual relationship. This might be very difficult and embarrassing at first, but you will be surprised how easy it becomes and how much help it is.

Sexual impotence in a man often begins when he fails to get an erection when drunk. This may make him anxious about his performance and this anxiety affects his performance even more. If, in addition to all this, his partner is resentful because he has drunkenly, insensitively and selfishly had sex without showing affection, and without caring enough about her feelings, her anger may make him feel even more insecure. This can result in impotence becoming long-lasting.

However, impotence may sometimes be quite easily remedied, although specialist help may be necessary. The key elements to overcoming this problem are showing affection, communicating and enjoying sexual preparation and foreplay without bothering too much about the end result. If you can do this, there is a good chance the problem will disappear.

These pointers apply to sexual problems in women also. However, if you are in any doubt, discuss your problems with your GP and he or she may be able to refer you to a sex problem clinic at the local hospital. In some areas, Marriage Guidance Councils also offer sexual counselling.

Here is a book that may help:

The Joy of Sex by **Alex Comfort. Published by Quartet Books.**

Insomnia

Quite a number of people use alcohol to help them sleep. If you take a small 'night-cap' which has stayed at the same amount for the last 10 years or so, then you need not worry too much. On the other hand, if you find that the amount you need to get you to sleep is gradually increasing, then watch out. Also, you should be aware that heavy drinking often causes sleep problems. Many of the methods for dealing with anxiety described on pages 105–110 may also be of use for insomnia. However, as with sexual problems, worries about performance often inhibit the performance itself. So if you lie awake at night worrying about not sleeping, then do the reverse! Go to bed and try not to sleep. Wait until you are tired before going to bed, even if this is 2 or 3 o'clock in the morning. Some people only need four or five hours sleep while some need nine or ten. Maybe you are trying to sleep more than you need to. Don't read, eat or watch TV in bed if you can't sleep. If you still have problems, see your doctor. The following book may be useful:

Stop Counting Sheep: Self-Help for Insomnia Sufferers **by Dr Paul Clayton. Published by Headline.**

Unemployment

Becoming unemployed means many things for a person – most of them stressful. It can mean isolation, boredom, poverty and not knowing what to do with your time. If you are already someone who tends to drink in response to stress, and especially if you receive redundancy money, then you run the risk of drinking heavily after losing your job.

Again, there are no easy answers to unemployment, but structuring your day so that you are not left with too much free time is one small step towards reducing the likelihood of heavy drinking. Trying to make sure that you find some way of meeting other people regularly – for instance, in a local unemployment resources centre, if there is one in your area – is another small step. Further advice is available in the following books:

How to Survice Without a Job by Ursula Markham. **Published by Piatkus Books.**

Beyond Redundancy by Christopher Bainton. **Published by Thorsons.**

'Craving' for alcohol

Do you sometimes feel a strong urge to drink? It may come out of the blue or it may appear predictably in certain situations or at certain times. Because craving can often feel like anxiety, you may crave alcohol when you are anxious. Boredom may also cause you to feel a strong urge to drink. What alternatives are there to drinking when you feel this urge to drink? Here are some suggestions.

Delay
Rather than drink immediately or soon after you feel the urge, delay your drinking for as long as you can. Sometimes when you do this, the urge to drink will pass. While you are delaying, you can also follow the second suggestion.

Distraction
Craving is partly to do with your mind focusing on thoughts and images of alcohol. If you change these thoughts you will stop craving, and the best way to change them is by distracting yourself. Choose some activity that you enjoy and which is easy to do without much preparation.

For instance, you could practise some relaxation methods (see page 107), or you might do some physical exercise if circumstances allow it. For some people, eating may have the desired effect, while others may find that listening to music, reading, watching TV or simply going for a walk would be enough to distract them from thoughts of drinking.

Or perhaps you might take a large, non-alcoholic drink, because sometimes thirst can be part of craving. If you have any hobbies or interests, immerse yourself in them for a while. If you do this, you will stand a good chance of reducing the craving. But the most important thing is to have some alternative activity planned and ready, so that you can recognize craving as it creeps up on you and nip it in the bud.

Thinking
Do you find yourself saying things to yourself like, 'I really need a drink'? If these thoughts go through your mind when you are craving alcohol, then they will make the craving worse.

These thoughts are irrational and false. You don't need a drink – you may want one but you don't need it. And why must you have a drink? The next time you feel a strong urge to drink at a time or place which conflicts with your Drinking Rules, try to pinpoint any such irrational thoughts which are running through your mind. Then challenge them logically. Replace them with 'I don't need a drink' or 'I don't have to drink' .

It is possible to change such thoughts, but it takes a lot of practice and the most difficult part is to pinpoint the irrational thoughts as they occur. If you succeed in replacing them with more rational thoughts, you will be a long way towards conquering craving.

Problem solving

Many people find that they drink more heavily when they run into problems and difficulties in their lives. Problems at home, problems with money, problems at work and many others can lead people to drink heavily.

Obviously, some of the methods discussed to do with finding alternative ways of coping with anxiety, depression and lack of confidence, will be of some use in coping with life's problems. However, sometimes by taking a detached view of the problem you may more readily find a solution to it.

Problem-solving skills training is a *systematic* way of approaching problems in general. Here are the steps to use.

- **1. Detach yourself from the problem.**
This is not easy, but try to pretend that you are an outside observer. Try to stop yourself reacting to problems by saying,

'Oh no, I can't cope', or, 'My life's a mess', or, 'What's the point, everything's against me'; because these thoughts bury you deeper in your problems and make it harder for you to see them clearly. Make believe you are an outside consultant called in to sort out the difficulties. Don't act impulsively. Wait and say to yourself something like 'I've got to stand back and look at this objectively'.

- **2. Spell out what the problems are.**
Be specific. Don't pass things off with vague phrases like 'My marriage is no good'. Instead, say more exactly what is wrong. For example, 'My wife complains that I never spend any time with her'. Or instead of saying 'I hate my job', spell out more precisely what the trouble with the job is, for example, 'I don't like my boss; he's always looking over my shoulder'.

- **3. Brainstorm for solutions.**
Remember on page 112 how you used brainstorming to come up with possible activities that you might enjoy. The principle is exactly the same here, only applied to solutions to a particular problem. Examples of a few solutions which might emerge from brainstorming on the 'I don't like the boss' problem are:

> **Leave the job.**
> **Ask the boss to leave you alone.**
> **Go out for a drink with him and talk things over.**
> **Ask for a transfer to another boss.**
> **Shout at him next time he seems to be pestering you.**
> **Complain to his superior.**
> **Ask him why he feels he has to watch you all the time.**
> **Get together with other employees and form a deputation.**
> **Ignore him and don't let it bother you.**

- **4. Decide on the best solution.** Having seen the problem in a fairly detached way and having come up with some possible solutions, now is the time to weed out the impractical solutions. Go over the most likely ones with a friend, clergyman or some other neutral person. Then decide on your best course of action.

121

- **5. Try out the solution.** But be ready to change the decision if, after a fair try, it appears not to be the right one. Where the solution requires you to do something which doesn't come easily, try to practise it in advance. For instance, if you have decided that you have to confront the boss, practise how you are going to set about it – either on your own or, preferably, with a friend or relative.

These very crude guidelines may be of some help to you in sorting out your problems, though not all problems have solutions. Where possible, try to work out your difficulties with some neutral person, because this makes it easier to achieve the detachment necessary for an effective solution. And don't bottle up your worries. Nowadays there are self-help groups for many different types of problem, ranging from compulsive gambling (Gamblers Anonymous) to bereavement (CRUSE). Ask at your Citizen's Advice Bureau if there is an organization catering for your needs in your area.

You can also check in a large bookshop where self-help books are available on many types of problem. Below are just three examples dealing with problems we have been unable to discuss in this chapter but which may be relevant to you.

Retirement. *The Which Guide to an Active Retirement.* Published by The Consumers' Association.
Family Problems. *Families and How to Survive Them* by Robin Skinner and John Cleese. Published by Cedar.
Tranquillizers. *How to Stop Taking Tranquillizers* by Dr. Peter Tyrer. Published by Sheldon.

Whatever your problems, never forget this simple fact:

Heavy drinking makes your problems worse!

9
SUPPOSE I HAVE A RELAPSE?

We have now come to the final chapter of this self-help guide. If you have read all the previous chapters carefully, if you have completed all the exercises we set you, if you have tried to put into practice all the advice we have given you, then you will be well on the way to achieving a lasting reduction in your drinking.

* * * * *

Congratulations! We bet you can feel the benefit already.

But hang on a moment! You are not out of the woods yet. And you must not become too confident about your new drinking habits.

The reason for saying this is that it is quite possible you are going to have a relapse – if indeed you have not already done so. By relapse, we simply mean one or more occasions when you will go over your Daily Cut-off or Weekly Grand Total and perhaps break some other of your Drinking Rules as well. As with any deeply-ingrained habit, *relapses into old drinking ways are common and you must expect them to occur.*

There are all kinds of reasons for a relapse. It might be the result of some special occasion which interferes with your new drinking behaviour, like going to a wedding or meeting an old friend you used to drink with. It might also be the result of some extra stress in your life which takes up too much emotional energy for you to worry about your drinking any more. There are many kinds of situation which might bring about a relapse.

The advice we gave you in Chapters 7 and 8 about methods to use in cutting down your drinking can be applied again if your drinking has increased. Just because you have had a relapse does not mean that you haven't made any progress.

One swallow doesn't make a summer

If you are learning to play a sport like golf, your progress will not be a steady improvement week by week. On some days you will play well, but on others you will think you are doing as badly as you did at the beginning. Does this mean that you have lost everything you ever learned on the golf course? Of course not! Learning is not smooth and unfaltering; it's a process of ups and downs.

Exactly the same applies to learning to cut down your drinking. Some days you may do badly and feel as if it's all a waste of time. You might feel that you have lost control over your habit. 'I'm back to square one', 'It's no use, I can't do it', 'I might as well be hanged for a sheep as a lamb' are perhaps some of the things you might find yourself thinking.

These statements are wrong. Yet the effect of thinking them is to make what you believe to be the case come true. Rather than brooding in this way, you should think of your relapse as just a 'slip' – as something you can put behind you and overcome.

The important thing is not to give up trying to cut down your drinking just because you have had a slip. You must stay calm and think carefully about the reasons for it. It is essential that you learn something from the experience. Then, the next time the kind of situation arises which brought about the slip, you will be ready for it and able to cope with it without heavy drinking.

Why not improve your drinking rules?

One way of learning from your experience is to improve the limits and rules you have fixed for your drinking. The Weekly Grand Total of 21 units for men and 14 for women is inflexible – you must not change that – but it is possible to change your Daily Cut-off point and your other Drinking Rules in the light of experience.

Obviously, we are not suggesting that you should change your rules every other day – that would destroy the point of the whole exercise. But if you find that you keep on going slightly over your Cut-off, then there might be a case for increasing it, bearing in mind the advice on setting your Daily Cut-off point given on page 91.

On the other hand, it might be that your Cut-off is too high and needs to be lowered. This may be because your Cut-off allows you to become too 'tipsy', so that you get in the mood for more alcohol and that is hard to resist. If this happens a number of times, try lowering your Cut-off to a point where you don't feel the effects of alcohol in this way.

You can also make improvements to your other Drinking Rules, like where, when and with whom you drink. Again, don't just change these rules on a whim. Give them a fair chance to see if they help you to cut down. But if you find from experience that there is something definitely wrong with one of your rules, then go ahead and improve it.

There is one time when you should definitely consider improving your Drinking Rules. This is after six weeks of filling in your Drinking Diary. In Chapter 7 you decided on your Drinking Rules after looking at four troublesome and four troublefree drinking occasions. But after keeping your Drinking Diary for six weeks, you will have a lot more information about your drinking which could be used to improve your Drinking Rules, if necessary. So it will be very useful to do the exercise all over again. Full details are given in Appendix C.

Change your attitude to drinking

Quite apart from occasional slips, when you may get drunk and break the rules you have set for yourself, there is another danger to be kept in mind. This is the danger of gradually slipping back into your bad old ways, almost without noticing it. We are talking here about a time scale of months, or even years. You may have been able to cut down your drinking now, but can you be sure that you will be able to keep up the good work in the months and years ahead?

Fortunately, there are things you can do to guard against this danger. As we advised you on page 81, you should continue to record your drinking in a pocket diary after finishing the Drinking Diary provided in this book. We suggest you get into the habit of jotting down your intake every day and that you keep this up for at least a year. After all, it only takes a few minutes of your time.

It is also important to calculate your Grand Total every week to make sure it isn't creeping up over the safe limit. You might consider recording this on a graph similar to the one given in Appendix D. This isn't much trouble and will be well worth the effort. (Graph paper is available at most stationers .)

In the longer term, however, keeping your drinking within safe limits is all about *an attitude of mind*. We sincerely hope that as a result of reading this book you will have become much more aware of your own drinking. You are thinking about it more and you understand it much better. What is now needed is for this new awareness to become a permanent part of your make-up. It should last you for the rest of your life. This change in attitude is the only way of making absolutely sure that you will never again drink regularly in a way which does you harm.

Suppose I haven't benefited from this book?

If you have reached this far in the book, most of you will have already achieved some success in cutting down your drinking. We are confident that most people who use this book and take it seriously will benefit from it.

There will be other people who have not benefited yet, but who will in the future. This is why you must give the methods described in the book a fair try and not give up too quickly. You should persevere with these methods for at least the 12 weeks covered by the Drinking Diary in Appendix B.

But there may be exceptions. There may be a few people, probably a very few, who will conscientiously use the book for three months or more, but who will not succeed in cutting down. There are many reasons why this might happen and there is no point in speculating about it here. It could be that you need specialized help, on a face-to-face basis, to help you get your drinking under control. It could even be that you are best advised to give up drinking completely.

In either case, you should seek specialized help for your problems from your nearest Council on Alcohol. They will advise you on your best course of action. So, if you have a drinking problem and if, after having given it a good try, you find that this book has not helped you, consult the list of addresses given in Appendix A.

Here's to your good health!

'I'll clear the way to the bar – you get the beer.'

APPENDIX A

LOCAL COUNCILS ON ALCOHOL AND ALCOHOL ADVISORY SERVICES

The following agencies have a wide range of policies for dealing with alcohol problems. Some may insist on abstinence, which, of course, may be necessary for some people whose drinking problems are severe.

ENGLAND

AVON
Avon Council on Alcohol & Drugs
14 Park Row
Bristol
BS1 5LJ
Tel: 0117 929 3028

BEDFORDSHIRE
Alcohol Services for the Community
(& South Bedfordshire CAT)
26-30 John Street
Luton
LU1 2JE
Tel: 01582-23434/29303

BERKSHIRE
West Berkshire Community Alcohol Service
Alcohol Advice Centre
342 Oxford Road
Reading
RG3 1AF
Tel: 01734-589557

BUCKINGHAMSHIRE
Buckinghamshire Council on Alcohol and
Drugs
Tindal Cottage
Bierton Road
Aylesbury
HP20 1EU
Tel: 01296-25329

Pegasus Drug & Alcohol Service
Cripps Lodge
Broadlands
Netherfield
Milton Keynes
MK6 4JJ
Tel: 01908-668603

CAMBRIDGESHIRE
Drinksense
Cambridge Alcohol Advisory Service
Head Office
79a Eastfield Road
Peterborough
PE1 4AS
Tel: 01733-555532

CHESHIRE
(Merseyside and Cheshire Alcohol Services)
Alcohol Services in Cheshire
Room 19, Breeden House
Edleston Road
Crewe
CW2 7EA
Tel: 01270-580243

CLEVELAND
Alcohol Counselling Service
The Albert Centre
3 Albert Terrace
Middlesborough
TS1 3PA
Tel: 01642-221484

CORNWALL
Cornwall Alcohol and Drug Agency Ltd
14 High Cross Street
St Austell
PL25 4AN
Tel: 01726-73984/67396

CUMBRIA
CADAS
Cumbria Alcohol and Drug Advisory Service
1 Fisher Street
Carlisle
CA3 8RR
Tel: 01288-44140

DERBYSHIRE
Southern Derbyshire
Alcohol Problems Advisory Service
1a College Place
Derby
DE1 3DY
Tel: 01332-345537

North Derbyshire Alcohol Advice Service
73 West Bars
Chesterfield
S40 1BA
Tel: 01246-206514/204344

DEVON
Insight Alcohol Services
Exeter Alcohol Advice & Counselling
59 Magdalen Street
Exeter
EX2 4HY
Tel: 01392-55151

Harbour Centre
9-10 Ermington Terrace
Mutley
Plymouth
PL4 6QG
Tel: 01752-267431

DORSET
Community Alcohol & Drugs Advisory Service
28 High West Street
Dorchester
DT1 1UP
Tel: 01305-265635/265901

DURHAM
North East Council on Addictions
Durham NECA Centre
Shakespeare Hall
North Road
Durham
County Durham
DH1 4SQ
Tel: 0191-383 0331

ESSEX
Alcohol & Drugs Advisory Service
118-120 The Stow
Harlow
CM20 3AS
Tel: 01279-641347
Helpline: 01279-438716

GLOUCESTERSHIRE
Alcohol Counselling and Information Service
15 Royal Crescent
Cheltenham
GL50 3DA
Tel: 01242-584881

HAMPSHIRE
OPTIONS Alcohol Counselling & Information
Service
147 Shirley Road
Southampton
SO15 2FH
Tel: 01703-630219

Alcohol Advisory Service
11a Stanley Street
Southsea
Portsmouth
PO5 2DS
Tel: 01705-296467

HEREFORD & WORCESTER
Hereford and Worcester Alcohol Advisory
Service
(South Worcestershire District)
10 Sansome Place
Worcester
Hereford & Worcester
WR1 1UA
Tel: 01905-27417

HERTFORDSHIRE
Hertfordshire Alcohol Problems Advisory
Service
St Anne's House
All Saints Pastoral Centre
Shenley Lane
London Colney
AL2 1AF
Tel: 01727-827677

Alcohol Advice Centre
2nd Floor
St Alban's House
181 The Parade
High Street
Watford, Herts
WD1 1NJ
Tel: 01923 221037

HUMBERSIDE
Hull and District Alcohol Advisory Service
82 Spring Bank
Hull
North Humberside
HU3 1AB
Tel: 01482-320606/7

Alcohol Counselling Service
11 New Street
Grimsby
South Humberside
DN31 1HQ
Tel: 01472-340001

ISLE OF WIGHT
Alcohol Advice Centre
19 Partlands Avenue
Ryde
Isle of Wight
PO33 3DS
Tel: 01983-566238

KENT
Kent Council on Addiction
Alcohol Advice Centre
41 Wincheap
Canterbury
CT1 3RX
Tel: 01227-454740

LANCASHIRE
(Greater Manchester and Lancashire Council
on Alcohol)
Alcohol Services (Lancashire)
81a Manchester Road
Preston
Lancashire
PR1 3YH
Tel: 01772-561300

LEICESTERSHIRE
Leicestershire Alcohol Advice Centre
70 London Road
Leicester
LE2 0QD
Tel: 0116-255 2212

LINCOLNSHIRE
Alcohol and Drugs Counselling Service
Portland House
3 Portland Street
Lincoln
LN5 7JZ
Tel: 01522-529222

LONDON
Alcohol Recovery Project
Central Office
68 Newington Causeway
Southwark
London
SE1 6DF
Tel: 0171-403 3369

Drink Crisis Centre
Central Office
107 Waterloo Road
London
SE1 8UL
Tel: 0171-401 3722

Greater London Association of Alcohol
Services
30-31 Great Sutton Street
London
EC1V 0DX
Tel: 0171-253 6221

MANCHESTER AND LANCASHIRE
Greater Manchester and Lancashire Regional
Council on Alcohol
Head Office
87 Oldham Street
Manchester
M4 1LW
Tel: 0161-834 9777

MERSEYSIDE AND CHESHIRE
Merseyside and Cheshire Alcohol Services
30 Hope Street
Liverpool
Merseyside
L1 9BX
Tel: 0151-707 1221

NORFOLK
Norfolk Community Alcohol Services
Parsonage Square Centre
11 Parsonage Square
Off School Lane
Norwich
NR2 1AS
Tel: 01603-660070

NORTHAMPTONSHIRE
Council on Addiction for Northamptonshire
81 St Giles Street
Northampton
NN1 1JF
Tel: 01604-27027

NOTTINGHAMSHIRE
Alcohol Problems Advisory Service
36 Park Row
Nottingham
NG1 6GR
Tel: 0115-941 4747
0345-626316 Lo-call

OXFORDSHIRE
Oxfordshire Council on Alcohol & Drug Use
Libra Project
St Lukes Church
Oxford Road, Cowley
Oxford
OX4 2EN
Tel: 01865-749800

SURREY
Surrey Alcohol & Drug Advisory Service
Head Office & South West Surrey Office
14 Jenner Road
Guildford
GU1 3PL
Tel: 01483-579313

SUSSEX
Sussex Alcohol Advice Service
82 Queens Road
Brighton
East Sussex
BN1 3XE
Tel: 01273-739147

TYNE & WEAR
North East Council on Addictions
Philipson House
3-5 Philipson Street
Walker
Newcastle-upon-Tyne
NE6 4EN
Tel: 0191-234 3486

WEST MIDLANDS
Alcohol Advisory Service
32 Essex Street
Birmingham
B5 4TR
Tel: 0121-622 2041

Alcohol Advisory Service (Coventry &
Warwickshire)
Swanswell House
Norton Street
Coventry
CV1 5FY
Tel: 01203-226619

Aquarius
Thornhurst
1 Connaught Road
Chapel Ash
Wolverhampton
WV1 4SJ
Tel: 01902-20041

WILTSHIRE
Wiltshire Council on Alcohol
Swindon Alcohol Advisory Centre
50 Victoria Road
Swindon
SN1 3AY
Tel: 01793-695405

YORKSHIRE
Leeds Addiction Unit
19 Springfield Mount
Leeds
West Yorkshire
LS2 9NG
Tel: 0113-292 6920

Unit 51
Pioneer House
53 Branch Road
Dewsbury
West Yorkshire
WF13 1AP
Tel: 01924-457038

Sheffield Alcohol Advisory Service
646 Abbeydale Road
Sheffield
South Yorkshire
S7 2BB
Tel: 0114-258 7553

Doncaster Agency on Alcohol Misuse
Alcohol Counselling Service
25 Bradford Row
Doncaster
South Yorkshire
DN1 3NF
Tel: 01302-368705

York & Selby Alcohol Advisory Service
63 Bootham
York
North Yorkshire
YO3 7BT
Tel: 01904-652104/610442
01757-213944

WALES

Alcohol Action Wales
4 Dock Chambers
Bute Street
Cardiff
CF1 6AG
Tel: 01222-488000

CLWYD & GWYNEDD
CAIS (Cyngor Alcohol Information Service)
111 High Street
Rhyl
Clwyd
LL18 1TR
Tel: 01745-343033

DYFED
Dyfed Alcohol Advisory Service
Forestry House
Brewery Road
Carmarthan
SA31 1TF
Tel: 01267-231634

GWENT
Trothny Housing Association Ltd
Ty Palmyra
3 Palmyra Place
Newport
NP9 4EJ
Tel: 01633-263185

MID GLAMORGAN
Mid Glamorgan Council on Alcoholism
Bryanawel House
Llanharry Road
Llanharan
CF7 9RN
Tel: 01443-226608

SOUTH GLAMORGAN
South Glamorgan Council on Alcohol
The Fitzhamon Centre
53b Fitzhamon Embankment
Riverside
Cardiff
CF1 8RN
Tel: 01222-388003

131

WEST GLAMORGAN
West Galmorgan Council on Alcohol and Drug Abuse
75 Uplands Crescent
Uplands
Swansea
SA2 0EX
Tel: 01792-472519

CHANNEL ISLANDS
The Guernsey Alcohol & Drug Abuse Council
Brockside
The Grange
St Peter Port
Guernsey
GY1 1RQ
Tel: 01481-723255

JERSEY
Community Alcohol and Drug Service
Catherine Quike House
2 Newgate Street
St Helier
Jersey
Tel: 01534-618110

SCOTLAND

Scottish Council on Alcohol
137-145 Sauchiehall Street
Glasgow
G2 3EW
Tel: 0141-333 9677

BORDERS
Borders Council on Alcohol
42 High Street
Galashiels
TD1 1SE
Tel: 01896-757657

CENTRAL
Central Scotland Council on Alcohol
4 Woodside Road
Stirling
FK8 1RF
Tel: 01786-450721

DUMFRIES & GALLOWAY
Dumfries and Galloway Council on Alcohol
190 King Street
Castle Douglas
DG7 1DB
Tel: 01556-503550

FIFE
Fife Council on Alcohol
28 North Street
Glenrothes
Fife
KY7 5NA
Tel: 01592-759543

GRAMPIAN
Alcohol Advisory & Counselling Service
62 Dee Street
Aberdeen
AB1 2DS
Tel: 01224-573887

Moray Council on Alcohol
80 High Street
Elgin
IV30 1BJ
Tel: 01343-545959

HIGHLANDS
Caithness Council on Alcohol
Rhind House Annexe
West Banks Avenue
Wick
KW1 5LU
Tel: 01955-603462

Inverness Area Council on Alcohol
106 Church Street
Inverness
IV1 1EP
Tel: 01463-220995

Lochaber Council on Alcohol
Caol Shopping Centre
Caol
Fort William
PH33 7DR
Tel: 01397-702340

Ross-shire Council on Alcohol
1 Mackay Street
Invergordon
Ross-shire
IV18 0DL
Tel: 01349-852438

Skye and Lochalsh Council on Alcohol
Highland Regional Council Offices
Dunvegan Road
Portree
Isle of Skye
IV51 9HD
Tel: 01478-612633

Sutherland Council on Alcohol
1 Duke Street
Golspie
Sutherland
KW10 6RP
Tel: 01408-634200

LOTHIAN
Edinburgh and Lothian Council on Alcohol
2nd Floor, 40 Shandwick Place
Edinburgh
EH2 4RT
Tel: 0131-225 8888

ORKNEY
Drinkwise Orkney
43 Junction Road
Kirkwall
Orkney
KW15 1AR
Tel: 01856-874738

SHETLAND
Alcohol Resource Centre
44 Commercial Street
Lerwick
Shetland
ZE1 0AB
Tel: 01595-5363

STRATHCLYDE
Ayrshire Council on Alcohol
2 Bridge Lane
Kilmarnock
KA1 1QH
Tel: 01563-541155

Cowal Council on Alcohol
4-6 Auchamore Road
Dunoon
Argyll
PA23 7DY
Tel: 01369-4406

Cumbernauld & Kilsyth Addiction Service
2nd Floor, Carron House
Town Centre
Cumbernauld
G67 1ER
Tel: Helpline 01236-735539
Office 01236-731378/738689

Dumbarton Area Council on Alcohol
West Bridgend Lodge
West Bridgend
Dumbarton
G82 4AD
Tel: 01389-731456

Glasgow Council on Alcohol
137-145 Sauchiehall Street
Glasgow
G2 3EW
Tel: 0141-353 2221

Inverclyde Council on Alcohol
Wellpark Centre
30 Regent Street
Greenock
PA15 4PB
Tel: 01475-785695/721325

Islay Council on Alcohol
Claddach Centre
Shore Street
Bowmore
Isle of Islay
PA43 7JS
Tel: 0149-810365

Kintyre Council on Alcohol
Castlehill
Campbeltown
Argyllshire
PA28 6AN
Tel: 01586-553555

Mid-Argyll Council on Alcohol
1 Argyll Street
Lochgilphead
Argyll
PA31 8LZ
Tel: 01546-602880

Monklands Council on Addictions
81C Hallcraig Street
Airdrie
ML9 6AN
Tel: 01236-753263

Oban Council on Alcohol
Room 2B
The Oban Times Building
The Esplanade
Oban
PA34 5PX
Tel: 01631-66090

Renfrew Council on Alcohol
Community Services Centre
Queen Street
Paisley
PA1 2TU
Tel: 0141-887 0880

TAYSIDE
Alcohol Advice and Information Centre
132A Nethergate
Dundee
DD1 4ED
Tel: 01382-223965

NORTHERN IRELAND

Northern Ireland Community Addiction
Service
40 Elmwood Avenue
Belfast
BT9 6AZ
Tel: 01232-664434/330499/731602

OTHER AGENCIES
Accept Services (UK)
724 Fulham Road
Hammersmith
London
SW6 5SE
Tel: 0171-371 7477/7555

Alcohol Concern
Waterbridge House
32-36 Loman Street
London
SE1 0EE
Tel: 0171-928 7377

133

Alcohol Counselling Services
Royal Hospital
Kew Foot Road
Richmond-upon-Thames
Surrey
TW9 2TE
Tel: 0181-940 7542/6529

Alcohol Recovery Project
Women's Alcohol Centre
66a Drayton Park
Islington
N5 1ND
Tel: 0171-266 4581

Aquarius
6th Floor
The White House
111 New Street
Birmingham
B2 4EU
Tel: 0121-632 4727

Aquarius Centre
Pebble Mill House
236 Bristol Road
Edgbaston
Birmingham
B5 7SL
Tel: 0121-471 1361

Aquarius Centre
4 St George's Street
Northampton
NN1 2TN
Tel: 01604 32421

Aquarius (Dudley Alcohol Services)
1st Floor, Molyneux Chambers
129-137 High Street
Brierly Hill
Dudley
West Midlands
DY5 3AU
Tel: 01384-261267/481976

Cedar Project
Community Alcohol and Drugs Team
Parkway Health Centre
Birdcroft Road
Welwyn Garden City
Hertfordshire
AL8 6JE
Tel: 01707-391000

Drug and Alcohol Women's Network
C/o GLAAS
30-31 Great Sutton Street
London
EC1V 0DX
Tel: 0171-253 6221

Ethnic Alcohol Counselling in Hounslow
(EACII)
Holdsworth House
65-67 Staines Road
Hounslow
Middlesex
TW3 3HW
Tel: 0181-577 6059

OPTIONS Shropshire Aquarius ACS
OPTIONS (Wellington)
48a Walker Street
Wellington
Telford
TF1 1BA
Tel: 01952-223165

Turning Point
New Loom House
101 Back Church Lane
London
E1 1LU
Tel: 0171-702 2300

ALCOHOLICS ANONYMOUS
England & Wales
Tel: 01904-644026

Scotland
Tel: 0141-221 9027

Northern Ireland
Tel: 01232-681084

Eire
Tel: 00 3531-453 8998

NATIONAL HELPLINE
DRINKLINE:
National Alcohol Helpline
Weddel House
7th Floor
13-14 West Smithfield
London
EC1A 9DL

Tel: 0171-332 0202 (Helpline London Area)
     0345-320202 (Helpline rest of UK)

SOS
There is also a recently-founded self-help
group called Secular Organizations for
Sobriety (SOS) which aims to help people
achieve sobriety without emphasizing spiri-
tual matters. Address: 28 Newgate Close, St
Albans, Herts, AL4 9JE; Phone: (01727)
851266.

APPENDIX B

Drinking diaries

The idea of keeping a Drinking Diary to record your drinking was explained to you in Chapter 7. There it was stressed that to get the maximum benefit from using this book, you must fill in your Drinking Diary every day. Preferably, you should fill it in as soon as possible after drinking while the memory of what you had is still fresh in your mind.

Remember that you can put both good and bad things down in the 'Consequences of Drinking' column. Remember also that you should try to record each drinking episode separately if there is more than one episode a day. Finally, remember to complete the diary for all 12 weeks provided and to add up the units for each week to make your weekly Grand Total. This, of course, should always be kept under 21 units for men and 14 units for women.

And in the unlikely event that you have forgotten: one unit = one half pint of beer = a single whisky = a glass of wine, etc. (Refer to the Conversion Table on page 13 to convert different drinks into standard units of alcohol.) Take care in estimating the number of units in drinks poured at home or at a friend's house because these often contain more than the usual pub measures.

Drinking Diary ——— WEEK 1

Day	Time	Hours spent	Place	Who with	Other activities	Money spent	Consequences (if any)	Units

TOTAL FOR WEEK

Drinking Diary ── WEEK 2

Day	Time	Hours spent	Place	Who with	Other activities	Money spent	Consequences (if any)	Units

TOTAL FOR WEEK

Drinking Diary — WEEK 3

Day	Time	Hours spent	Place	Who with	Other activities	Money spent	Consequences (if any)	Units

TOTAL FOR WEEK

Drinking Diary — WEEK 4

Day	Time	Hours spent	Place	Who with	Other activities	Money spent	Consequences (if any)	Units

TOTAL FOR WEEK

Drinking Diary — WEEK 5

Day	Time	Hours spent	Place	Who with	Other activities	Money spent	Consequences (if any)	Units

TOTAL FOR WEEK

140

Drinking Diary

WEEK 6

Day	Time	Hours spent	Place	Who with	Other activities	Money spent	Consequences (if any)	Units

TOTAL FOR WEEK

141

Drinking Diary

WEEK 7

Day	Time	Hours spent	Place	Who with	Other activities	Money spent	Consequences (if any)	Units

TOTAL FOR WEEK

142

Drinking Diary —— WEEK 8

Day	Time	Hours spent	Place	Who with	Other activities	Money spent	Consequences (if any)	Units

TOTAL FOR WEEK

Drinking Diary

WEEK 9

Day	Time	Hours spent	Place	Who with	Other activities	Money spent	Consequences (if any)	Units

TOTAL FOR WEEK

Drinking Diary — WEEK 10

Day	Time	Hours spent	Place	Who with	Other activities	Money spent	Consequences (if any)	Units

TOTAL FOR WEEK

145

Drinking Diary

WEEK 11

Day	Time	Hours spent	Place	Who with	Other activities	Money spent	Consequences (if any)	Units

TOTAL FOR WEEK

146

Drinking Diary

WEEK 12

Day	Time	Hours spent	Place	Who with	Other activities	Money spent	Consequences (if any)	Units

TOTAL FOR WEEK

Troublesome Drinking Times

	Day/ Date	Time	Hours Spent	Place	Who with	Other Activities	Units	Money Spent	Consequences (if any)
TIME 1									
TIME 2									
TIME 3									
TIME 4									

Trouble Free Drinking Times

	Day/ Date	Time	Hours Spent	Place	Who with	Other Activities	Units	Money Spent	Consequences (if any)
TIME 1									
TIME 2									
TIME 3									
TIME 4									

APPENDIX C

Revised drinking rules

After six weeks of keeping your Drinking Diary you will have a lot of information on the way you drink. You should therefore repeat the exercise first set you on page 88 – the exercise aimed at making a set of personal Drinking Rules.

Look over your Drinking Diary and find the last four occasions when drinking caused you trouble – in other words, occasions when you went over your Daily Cut-off point or broke some other rule. When you have done this, copy down the information. (Don't worry if you can't find four troublesome drinking occasions: put down as many as you have. If you can't find any troublesome occasions, there is no need to do this exercise.)

Now find four occasions when you drank without any trouble and kept within your limit. Copy the information down.

* * * * *

Now see whether there is anything common to the first four occasions and anything common to the second four. Write down these common features. Write as many or as few as you can find. (Don't worry if you can only find one or two.)

You are now in a position to change your Drinking Rules if necessary. Refer back to page 81 for a full explanation of how to arrive at your Drinking Rules and then write any changed rules you think are necessary in the box provided.

What do my troublesome drinking sessions have in common?

1.

2.

3.

4.

5.

What do my trouble free drinking sesions have in common?

1.

2.

3.

4.

5.

Now fill in 'My Revised Drinking Rules' on the next page.

My Revised Drinking Rules

1.

2.

3.

4.

5.

APPENDIX D

Drinking graph

As we explained in Chapter 7, a very good way of rewarding your success in cutting down drinking is to be able to see at a glance the progress you have made on a graph. This will also be useful as a warning if you start to slide back into your bad drinking habits.

Keeping a Drinking Graph is really simple. All you have to do is note how much you have drunk each week – the weekly Grand Total from the Drinking Diary in Appendix B – and then put a small cross on the appropriate column in the Graph. It would be best to make a note of the date underneath the column on which you record your Grand Total. As you put a cross for your Grand Total each week, join the crosses up with straight lines until you have completed the 12 weeks of the graph. (Note that there are lines already drawn across the graph to represent the weekly limits for men and women respectively.)

Now sit back and admire the way the line charting your drinking is going steadily down or at least keeping to a safe and healthy level. If the line starts going up again, and especially if it goes over the recommended limit, ask yourself what has happened to your drinking and then do something about it. Go back to Chapters 7 and 8 and read them again

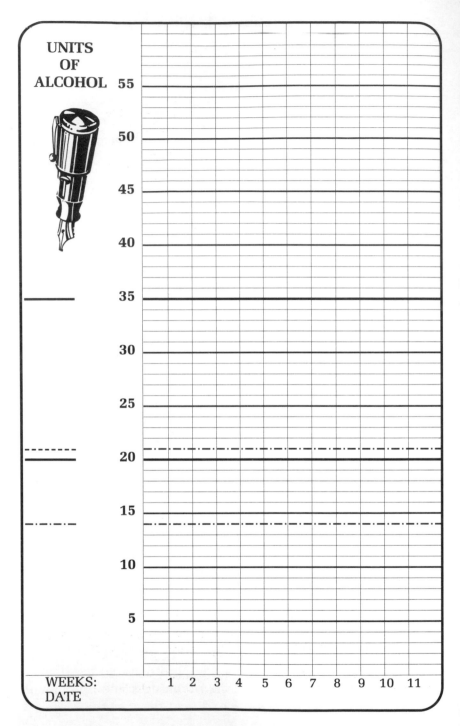

UNITS
OF
ALCOHOL   55

50

45

40

35

30

25

20

15

10

5

WEEKS: 1   2   3   4   5   6   7   8   9   10 11
DATE

152

Index